I Stand on Holy Ground

Other *Writings of* JOEL S. GOLDSMITH

Living by the Word

Living the Illumined Life

Seek Ye First

Spiritual Discernment

A Message for the Ages

I Stand on Holy Ground

The Art of Spiritual Living

God Formed Us for His Glory

The Journey Back to His Father's House

Showing Forth the Presence of God

The Only Freedom

The Infinite Way

Practicing the Presence

The World Is New

Consciousness Transformed

God The Substance of All Form

Man Was Not Born to Cry

Living Now

Consciousness Is What I Am

Gift of Love

The Art of Meditation

The Altitude of Prayer

The Contemplative Life

Conscious Union with God

The Art of Spiritual Healing

The Spiritual Power of Truth

The Thunder of Silence

Awakening Mystical Consciousness

Realization of Oneness

A Parenthesis In Eternity

Living Between Two Worlds

Rising In Consciousness

Consciousness In Transition

Our Spiritual Resources

Living the Infinite Way

The Master Speaks

Beyond Words and Thoughts

Leave Your Nets

Consciousness Unfolding

Spiritual Interpretation of Scripture

The Foundation of Mysticism

The Early Years

1954 Infinite Way Letters

1955 Infinite Way Letters

1956 Infinite Way Letters

1957 Infinite Way Letters

1958 Infinite Way Letters

1959 Infinite Way Letters

The Heart of Mysticism:1955-1959

The Mystical I

I STAND ON HOLY GROUND

Joel S. Goldsmith

Edited by
Lorraine Sinkler

Acropolis Books, Publisher
Longboat Key, Florida

For Information Contact:
Acropolis Books, Inc.
Longboat Key, Florida
www.acropolisbooks.com

Library of Congress Cataloging-in-Publication Data

Goldsmith, Joel S., 1892-1964.
 I stand on holy ground / Joel S. Goldsmith ; edited by Lorraine
Sinkler.
  p. cm.
  Includes bibliographical references (p.   0.
  ISBN 978-188905-165-9
  1.   Spiritual Life. I. Sinkler, Lorraine. II. Title.

BP610.G64155   2003
299'.93—dc21
                                          2003013243

Except the Lord build the house,
they labour in vain that build it. . .

– Psalm 127

⌒

"Illumination dissolves all material ties and binds men together with the golden chains of spiritual understanding; it acknowledges only the leadership of the Christ; it has no ritual or rule but the divine, impersonal universal Love; no other worship than the inner Flame that is ever lit at the shrine of Spirit. This union is the free state of spiritual brotherhood. The only restraint is the discipline of Soul; therefore, we know liberty without license; we are a united universe without physical limits, a divine service to God without ceremony or creed. The illumined walk without fear – by Grace."

–The Infinite Way by Joel S. Goldsmith

Dedication

Twentieth century mystic Joel S. Goldsmith revealed to the Western world the nature and substance of mystical living that demonstrated how mankind can live in the consciousness of God. The clarity and insight of his teachings, called the Infinite Way, were captured in more than thirty-five books and in over twelve hundred hours of tape recordings that, today, perpetuate his message.

Joel faithfully arranged to have prepared from his class tapes, monthly letters which were made available as one of the most important tools to assist students in their study and application of the Infinite Way teachings. He felt each of these letters came from an ever-new insight that would produce a deeper level of understanding and awareness of truth as students worked diligently with this fresh and timely material.

Each yearly compilation of the *Letters* focused on a central theme, and it became apparent that working with an entire year's material built an ascending level of consciousness. The *Letters* were subsequently published as books, each containing all the year's letters. The publications became immensely popular as they proved to be of great assistance in the individual student's development of spiritual awareness.

Starting in 1954, the monthly letters were made availiable to students wishing to subscribe to them. Each year of the *Letters* was published individually during 1954 through 1959 and made available in book form. From 1960 through 1970 the *Letters* were published and renamed as books with the titles:

1960 Letters	*Our Spiritual Resources*
1961 Letters	*The Contemplative Life*
1962 Letters	*Man Was Not Born to Cry*
1963 Letters	*Living Now*
1964 Letters	*Realization of Oneness*
1965 Letters	*Beyond Words and Thoughts*
1966 Letters	*The Mystical I*
1967 Letters	*Living Between Two Worlds*
1968 Letters	*The Altitude of Prayer*
1969 Letters	*Consciousness Is What I Am*
1970 Letters	*Awakening Mystical Consciousness*

Joel worked closely with his editor, Lorraine Sinkler, to ensure each letter carried the continuity, integrity, and pure consciousness of the message. After Joel's transition in 1964, Emma A. Goldsmith (Joel's wife) requested that Lorraine continue working with the monthly letters, drawing as in the past from the inexhaustible tape recordings of his class work with students. The invaluable work by Lorraine and Emma has ensured that this message will be preserved and available in written form for future generations. Acropolis Books is honored and privileged to offer in book form the next eleven years of Joel's teaching.

The 1971 through 1981 *Letters* also carry a central theme for each year, and have been renamed with the following titles:

1971 Letters	*Living by the Word*
1972 Letters	*Living the Illumined Life*
1973 Letters	*Seek Ye First*
1974 Letters	*Spiritual Discernment: the Healing Consciousness*
1975 Letters	*A Message for the Ages*
1976 Letters	*I Stand on Holy Ground*
1977 Letters	*The Art of Spiritual Living*
1978 Letters	*God Formed Us for His Glory*
1979 Letters	*The Journey Back to the Father's House*
1980 Letters	*Showing Forth the Presence of God*
1981 Letters	*The Only Freedom*

Acropolis Books dedicates this series of eleven books to Lorraine Sinkler and Emma A. Goldsmith for their ongoing commitment to ensure that these teachings will never be lost to the world.

Table of Contents

1 Living the Spiritual Life

17 From Practicing the Presence to the Prayer of Listening

35 Meditation, the Door to Fulfillment

53 The Stature of Spiritual Manhood

71 Nothing Takes Place Outside of Consciousness

89 I, If I Be Lifted Up

105 A Lesson On Grace

123 Spiritual Supply

141 Cast Thy Bread on the Waters

157 The New Dispensation

173 Self-Purification, the Way to the Mystical Consciousness

189 The Ye-Shall-Know-the-Truth Way

207 About the Series

209 Scriptural References and Notes

215 Tape Recording References

I Stand on Holy Ground

Chapter One

Living the Spiritual Life

The spiritual way of life is a practical way of life, perhaps the most practical way that has ever been known. It can be lived in the midst of war, in the midst of shifting economic conditions, and in a world filled with a great deal of suffering and lack in some parts, and in others filled with too much prosperity for the good of those who are seemingly enjoying it.

It has been thought by some that the spiritual life can be lived successfully only by those who are in a position to retire from active business or professional life, those who would live away from the world in the mountains or by the sea. But contrary to popular belief the spiritual life is not only most necessary but also most practical and profitable during the stresses and strains of everyday living.

The spiritual life is in no way dependent upon a religious life in the church sense. It has no greater connection with the religious life than it has with business or professional life. Yet by its very nature it can be lived in the church, in the business or professional world, or in a combination of these.

The Presence of God Realized Is Your Security

Spiritual living has to do with man and his relationship with God. A person can have that relationship with God on a battlefield, in an airplane, or on a barren desert island. What is necessary is a person's ability to find his center in God, whether he finds it in or out of church. If he has not found God within himself, all the churches in the universe cannot save him.

The spiritual life can be thought of as a person's individual experience of God. If you cannot find the kingdom of God within yourself, wherever you may be—in your home, in your automobile, or on a holiday—you will not find it in your house of worship because a church, a temple, a mosque, or a synagogue is merely a building, a place. The kingdom of God is within you, and in order to find God wherever you are you must bring the awareness of God there, and whether you travel by automobile, train, ship, or plane, you must remember that you carry the kingdom of God with you.

Every day the newspapers, television, and radio are filled with accounts of automobile, train, ship, and airplane accidents and fatalities. But there is just as much of God in the plane, in the ship, or in the car as there is in any holy mountain or holy temple, and therefore, there is just as much security, just as much safety in the plane, on the battlefield, or in an automobile as there is in a church.

When you are called upon to use transportation of any kind, where the threat of danger lurks or insecurity exists, you will find your security by carrying with you the realization that the place where you stand is holy ground and that no accident or danger of any kind can come near your dwelling place, which is your consciousness. Accidents take place when there is no realization of the presence of God. God, when realized as omnipresence, the divine presence where you are, makes it impossible for any of the evils of this world to reach you.

It is not because of God's omnipresence that you are safe and secure in the midst of danger: but because of your *conscious realization, recognition,* and *acknowledgment* of God's presence that you bring safety, security, and peace wherever you may be.

Live Consciously in the Presence of God

Pray without ceasing.
I Thessalonians 5:17.

Where the Spirit of the Lord is,
there is liberty.
II Corinthians 3:17

In all thy ways acknowledge him, and
he shall direct thy paths.
Proverbs 3:6

The spiritual life demands that you live consciously aware of the presence of God, from morning to night, and from night to morning, not taking it for granted, not glibly saying, "Oh, yes, God fills all space." Hour by hour, moment by moment, some conscious realization must take place within you that where you are, God is and that you and the Father are one, inseparable and indivisible. The spiritual life consists of consciously and constantly abiding in this Word, constantly and consciously remembering the presence of God, even though God may seem to be absent.

An experience took place some years ago in my life, when a group of persons involved in spiritual work went into a restaurant to find that the only table available was directly in front of the bar. One of the members of the group was quite shocked at the thought of sitting at this table. But one person raised the question,

"Why not?"

"Because this is a den of iniquity."

"I thought that God was everywhere equally present, and if God is, I cannot possibly see how a den of iniquity could exist. In fact, I do not see one: I see a table set ready for us to eat, and I see each one of us as spiritually minded people about the

Father's business. I do not think what our neighbor is doing should concern us except that we should be blessing him and asking the Father to open his eyes, if his eyes are not yet opened." The group enjoyed their dinner and left without feeling any of the iniquity that was supposed to be there.

There are times and places, however, when events might transpire to cause you to feel that God could not be in a certain place. The answer is that such a condition could exist only because God was not realized in that place, for "where the spirit of the Lord is," none of these things can exist. None of the evils of the world can enter the consciousness of those who abide in the Word.

The Withering Branch

Abide in me, and I in you. As the branch
cannot bear fruit of itself, except
it abide in the vine; no more can ye,
except ye abide in me.

If a man abide not in me, he is cast
forth as a branch and is withered.

John 15:4,6

When you see the withering branches—sinning and suffering humanity—you know that right there, there has been an absence of a realization of God's presence, a failure to "pray without ceasing," and probably an ignorance of the fact that such conditions can exist only where the conscious recognition of God is absent.

"Where the spirit of the Lord is, there is liberty," but where is the spirit of the Lord? Paul reminds us that as human beings we are not under the law of God, cannot please God, have no God-protection, no God-support, and no God-healing. But if the spirit of God dwells in us, then do we become children of

God, "and if children, then heirs: heirs of God"[1] to all the heavenly riches—peace, harmony, wholeness, completeness, safety, security. It is folly to hope that man will come under the grace or the law of God until he permits the spirit of God consciously to dwell in him, so that he may become the son and heir of God.

To the son of God, the promise is "Son, thou art ever with me, and all that I have is thine."[2] But that was not said to the human race because the human race has none of it. Only as a person comes out from the world, becomes separate, and permits the spirit of God to dwell in him does he become the child of God, heir of God. Then he is under the law, the protection, and the sustaining power of God.

The scriptures of all peoples agree that where God is consciously maintained in individual thought, there is the peace of God, the grace of God, and the joy of God, but where this conscious awareness is absent, there is no evidence of God's power or presence. The Old Testament teaches that the Word must be in the forehead, bound on the arm, and posted at the doorway of one's home. In other words, the name of God, the presence, the activity and the acknowledgment of God must constantly be before you so that you do not forget it.

The Difficulty of Simplicity

It is easy to understand why the spiritual life has been so difficult for a person to achieve. It is far too simple, so simple that the answer often is, "It is too good to be true." If it were something complex or something people had to memorize or stand on their heads to achieve, more people would achieve it. Human beings value or appreciate being complex or doing the impossible, but studying the fifteenth chapter of John or reading the twenty-second chapter of Luke, verses twelve to twenty-two, is too simple. "Take no thought for your life."[3] Isn't that simple? No affirmations, nothing to study, nothing to read, just "take no thought for your life." Why?

There is God and this God knows your need. God not only knows your need, but it is His pleasure to give you the kingdom. For most persons that is too simple. There must be some more difficult way to attain God than to take no thought and to believe that because there is a God, Its nature must be intelligence and love. With that intelligence, It knows our need, and with love as Its nature It provides for this need.

The spiritual life is that simple! It is a matter of consciously remembering that you need take no thought for your life, but rather spend your time taking care of your business, profession, or your household, and rejoice that God knows your need before you do and that it is His good pleasure to give you all good. Living the spiritual life consists of the ability to take no anxious thought, have no concern, no doubt, no fear, in the realization that if God is, God must be of the nature of intelligence and love, and above all things, God must be omnipresent. God must be where you are whether you mount up to heaven or temporarily make your bed in hell, and you can find Him anywhere because He is everywhere. You fear no evil, for God is omnipresence. If God is not omnipresence, there is no God.

Abide in the realization that neither life nor death can separate you from the love of God.

> For I am persuaded, that neither death, nor life, nor
> angels, nor principalities, nor powers, nor things
> present, nor things to come,
>
> Nor height, nor depth, nor any other creature,
> shall be able to separate us from the love of God,
> which is in Christ Jesus our Lord.
> Romans 8:38,39

Neither life—any form of life, any manifestation of life, any place where life may be lived—neither life nor death can separate you from the love of God. How simple it is to be able to rest and relax in that assurance! Nothing, not sin and not disease, can separate you from the love of God, and there can be sin and disease only if you forget God, not because God has forgotten you.

The Father Awaits Your Return

The Prodigal Son left home and became a beggar because he wandered away from his father. His father did not forsake him. All the time his father was waiting for his return, waiting to greet him with the royal robe and the jeweled ring. So it is with your heavenly Father that is within you. This Father you have left is "closer. . . than breathing," awaiting your return. Return where? You do not have to go any place; you do not have to leave the seat you are sitting in, for the Father is neither here nor there, but within you. It is merely a matter of turning within.

> Father, you have been here all the time, but I have
> been out visiting. I have experienced eating with the
> swine. I have experienced sin and found it not at all
> pleasurable. I have experienced dishonesty, lack of
> integrity, and found it took me exactly nowhere. I
> have experienced a loss of faith and found that even
> that did not harm me. Now I am coming home,
> home to the home within me, in the realization that
> where I am, Thou art, because of omnipresence. If at
> a given moment I find myself in heaven, Thou art
> there, but in this temporary hell in which I find
> myself, there Thou art also. If I am walking "through
> the valley of the shadow of death,"⁴ Thou art there;
> for where I am, Thou art.

> Now that I am home in Thee, I have nothing further
> to seek or attain—not employment, not
> companionship, not supply—because now that I am
> home, I hear those magic words: "Son, thou art ever

with me, and all that I have is thine."
All! All! Peace, security, abundance, companionship,
joy, purity, healing, restoration
of the lost years of the locust,
resurrection, if necessary.
"All that I have is thine."

And the simplicity continues! Live consciously in the realization: All that the Father has is mine. Be patient while the outer circumstances begin to adjust, and sometimes slowly, sometimes quickly, you are restored in your whole mind, abiding again in the Spirit. Then never again let go, because you are warned by the Master: "Behold, thou art made whole: sin no more, lest a worse thing come unto thee."[5]

You have discovered now that by abiding in the conscious realization of God's presence, realizing that the Father is within and that you need take no thought for your life, you witness the good flowing into your experience. Do not go back merely to enjoying the good and forget the source of the good. Forgetting the source of the good in the enjoyment of the good itself is a major sin.

A Daily Program of
Conscious Realization

To those who have been accustomed to thinking of God only once in a great while, it may be a little difficult to begin a program of conscious realization. It can be done, however, and it is the foundation of our work in the Infinite Way where it is made clear that you are to begin on waking up in the morning, before you get out of bed, to have several minutes for quiet contemplation of the truth of God's presence, God's grace, God's law, and God's abundance, of God as your sufficiency.

At breakfast, acknowledge God as the source of all that appears, not only on your table, but on all the tables of the world, for God has not put anything specifically on your table: God has put it on the earth for everyone's table. God does not produce ham and eggs for *your* breakfast: the ham and eggs in the world have no name on them. They are for those who attain the consciousness of God's presence, if they will have it so.

God's grace is never directed to you or me: God's grace is directed to those who have the spirit of God dwelling in them, and it is available to any and all who will open themselves to it. So you go through your day acknowledging God's grace.

> But for the grace of God
> I could not manage my
> business or my profession successfully.
> But for the grace of God my business
> would not be as good,
> satisfactory, or successful as it is.
> God is the cement of my human relationships,
> that which unites me with all with whom I meet.

Branches of the Tree of Life

God is your life and my life. There is no separate life for the orchid, the potato, or for the orange: there is but one Life. There is no separate life in me and in you: it is the same Life flowing in everyone. There is no Jewish life, Protestant life, Catholic life, Taoist life, or Vedantist life: there is only one Life expressing as everyone. There is no white life, yellow life, or black life: there is one Life, and because of this one Life, we are one.

Many sincere religious persons have been reluctant to accept the truth that they are branches of the one Tree of Life. The truth is that if God is the Tree of Life, everyone is a branch— you are a branch and I am a branch, regardless of color, race, or to what church a person belongs or does not belong.

In the materialistic way of life you consider yourself as one person and you have thought of me a separate person, and that what affects you does not affect me or what affects me does not affect you. There are those who even believe that they can deprive others of something and still benefit themselves. All this is nonsense. In the relationship of the Tree of Life and the branches, whatever benefits one must benefit all. Whatever hurts one must hurt all.

"Inasmuch as ye have done it unto one of the least of these my brethren, ye have done it unto me."[6] You can adopt this as a spiritual way of life by realizing: Whatever I do, even unto the least of these in the world, I am doing unto myself. Whatever of good or of evil I do unto the least of these I am doing unto myself, for there is but one Self. The self of me is the self of you, the life of me is the life of you, the mind of me is the mind of you. There is but one mind, one life, one soul, one spirit, and even the body is one.

As we look at a tree, with its trunk, roots, and branches, we see one tree, one form, one body. We do not think that each branch has a body of its own. There is one body, the body of the tree, and the body of the tree includes everything, from the roots up to the outermost tip of every branch. It is one tree, and so are we.

We are one Tree of Life. God is the life-force of It; we are the branches, all fed and all receiving our grace from the same source, and whatever is flowing from God to bless one branch blesses every branch. All branches do not receive it because they have shut themselves off at the connecting link, and the connecting link is knowing the truth that makes free.

So if I declare that there is a Tree of Life, which is God, and that all of us are the branches, and are one, whatever I wish for myself I wish for every branch, and whatever I would wish done to me I do unto any and every branch that comes within range of my consciousness. If I do this and abide in it, I am knowing the truth that makes me free from lack, limitation, hatred, enmity, jealousy, danger, evil, and from the plots and plans of men.

Every branch, that is, every individual, has available the

entire grace of God, but only by consciously knowing the truth that we are one in God and that everyone derives his good from the Source. It is the knowing that makes free.

Sowing and Reaping

Spiritual living, then, is a knowing of the truth, but not just knowing the truth in order to meet a problem. Constantly and consciously knowing your relationship with God and with one another is knowing the truth. This is spiritual living. Notice what it does to you when you realize that every good you do, even unto the least person, you are doing unto yourself and that the least injury or injustice you do to another, you are visiting upon yourself.

Christian scripture makes very clear that "whatsoever a man soweth, that shall he also reap."[7] Whatever you are thinking or doing, you are doing unto yourself. In knowing an untruth about another, that is, in malpracticing another, you are really doing it unto yourself. It is a matter of sowing and reaping. The injustice, the impatience, the intolerance that you express, you are doing to yourself.

"He that soweth to his flesh shall of the flesh reap corruption."[8] If the truth about that statement were taught, which is not very often, we would know how to obey it. Ordinarily it is thought that sowing to the flesh and reaping corruption means indulging in some bodily sin. Be assured that the author of that statement never even thought of bodily sin in connection with it. What that statement means is that if you think of your neighbor as being material, physical, or evil, you are sowing to the flesh, and you will reap corruption. If you are dwelling in the realization of your neighbor as being of the same spiritual household as yourself, under the grace of God, you are sowing to the Spirit. Whenever you are knowing a spiritual truth, you are sowing to the Spirit, and you will reap life everlasting. Any time that you accept materiality for anyone, including yourself, you are sowing to the flesh and will reap corruption.

Sow to the Spirit by knowing that there is but one God. That God is Spirit, the Tree of Life, and everyone is a branch of that one Tree: saints and sinners alike. The sinner, at the moment, does not know it, and that is what makes him a sinner. When he awakens to his true identity, he is no longer a sinner.

The Master proved that truth by not holding the woman taken in adultery in condemnation. He knew that she, also, was a branch of the same Tree of which he was a branch, but that she was in ignorance of it. Therefore, he did not condemn her, but rather loosed and freed her by realizing, "You are a daughter of the most High. Now act that way. 'Go, and sin no more.'" [9] He not only released her from the penalties of her sins and brought about her reformation, but he brought upon himself the grace of God, because he had sowed to the Spirit and, therefore, reaped of the Spirit. This, too, is spiritual living: knowing the truth about your neighbor, even the truth about your enemy neighbor.

Praying for the Enemy

Regardless of how much praying you do for your friends, you are not children of God until you take up the practice of praying for your enemies. Spiritual living is making your first prayer of the day a prayer for your enemies. Whether you are thinking in terms of personal enemies, national enemies, or world enemies, it makes no difference. You have to pray that their souls be opened. Then, when you have finished your prayer for your enemies, you can begin your prayer for your friends or relatives, but not before. The praying for friends and relatives is of little profit until you have fulfilled your function as children of God.

Can you not see that if, by the grace of God, you were touched with a healing grace, and you decided you would help only the good people in the world or the people who belong to your religion or your race, you would soon lose that healing gift? No one has ever been given a healing gift to use just for his friends, his children, or his relatives. When the grace of God bestows a healing gift upon anyone, it is meant that anyone who turns to spiritual healing for himself will find that you are a light unto him.

As an instrument for spiritual healing, you soon learn that you are called upon to heal those you do not like, those you think deserve it, and those you think do not deserve it. You may be called upon to heal more sinners than saints, and if you do not have the consciousness that can do that, you will not have the healing consciousness for long.

Know the Truth

Sinners, tyrants, dictators are not what they are because they are bad, but because they are ignorant that the grace of God is their sufficiency in all things. No man could be a thief, a tyrant, a liar, or a cheat if he knew the truth that "My grace is sufficient for thee."[10] It would be impossible, for what more is there in this world to be gained than the grace of God could give one?

It has been said, "Ye shall know the truth, and the truth shall make you free."[11] What truth? "My grace is sufficient for thee." There is no need then to lie, cheat, steal, or defraud, beg, or even borrow, once the realization has dawned within: Thy grace—not the bank at the corner, not the loan agency, not the government, not the social security system, but Thy grace—is sufficient in all things. It is not my husband's good will, my wife's good will, my mother's or my father's good will, but Thy grace that is sufficient for me.

You are never really freed of lack or limitation until you have learned inwardly to stop being dependent on "man, whose breath is in his nostrils"[12] and come to the realization that "My grace is sufficient for thee."

In proportion as you accept God as omnipotence, germs,

infection, contagion, paralysis, drought, and tornadoes will be robbed of power. By accepting the truth that these are but the "arm of flesh,"[13] temporal power, non-power, it will be made evident that God is omnipotent and nothing else is power.

The spiritual life, then, is based on knowing the truth. That is how simple it is: knowing the truth given in the scriptures of the world. In all of them, the source of scripture is the divine consciousness, whether revealed through a Hebrew prophet, a Christian prophet, a Mohammedan prophet, or any other prophet. The source of all truth is the same, and those who write it or voice it are but the instruments of that source.

Each one of them has revealed that by abiding in the Word and letting the Word abide in you, you bear fruit richly. By not abiding in the Word and not letting the Word abide in you, you are a branch of a tree that is cut off and withers.

An Important Requirement for Living the Spiritual Life

Is it possible for everyone to live the spiritual life? Yes, provided a person has the desire. Without that desire, it is impossible because the spiritual life makes certain demands that those who have no desire for it can never fulfill.

There are those who by nature or temperament are not prepared for the spiritual life, but anyone with the desire can live the spiritual life and eventually will, if he is able to give up that localized and finite concept of God, and accept God as the principle, the creator, and the Father of all men, whether Jew or Gentile, white or black.

One of the first things you must have before you can live the spiritual life is a God whom you acknowledge to be the God of all equally. This does not mean that God will bring health, safety, security, and peace into the lives of all men. It means that God is equally everywhere present, but God's grace comes to you only as you open yourself and permit that spirit of God to dwell in you.

Let Go of False Concepts of God

You must give up all belief in a God who punishes and rewards. Would not such a God be but a human being? There is no such God. This does not mean that there is no punishment nor does it mean that there is no reward. If life teaches us anything at all, it is that there are both, but God has nothing to do with either. The punishment and the reward come from our own sowing which determines the reaping.

What God has been, God is now, and what God is now, God will ever be. God is flowing forth as life, love, being, immortality, and eternality. God cannot begin to do that for you tomorrow. God is forever being.

You can begin to avail yourself of all that God is, and you can begin with this very minute. There are those who would prefer to put it off until next year or until sometime when disease or poverty has engulfed them. But when they are willing to turn with their whole heart, soul, and mind, in that instant they are made "white as snow."[14]

When you surrender yourself and come to the realization of any errors you may have been guilty of, you are cleansed, and from then on, you live under God's grace, not because God's grace began that moment, but because you had been shutting yourself off from God's grace and in your turning, you offer and return yourself to It. God never shuts Himself off from you: you shut yourself off from God. God's grace is available this instant. Only "turn yourselves, and live ye."[15]

If you live, move, and have your being in God awareness, if you dwell consciously in the presence of God, if you hold God as the law and life of your being, there is a peace that goes out from you, and it is felt by those with whom you come in contact. On the other hand, those who live a grasping, mean, unkind life broadcast that, too, and everyone who comes near them knows it.

To live the spiritual life means to begin to understand the

nature of God. Then you will have a God that you can love with all your heart and mind and soul, one you do not have to fear, and you will have neighbors you can love as your Self.

ACROSS THE DESK

This month's letter is an important one and, therefore, a good way in which to begin the New Year. As you study it, think how different your experience would be if every day you applied the truth set forth in this lesson. How many of you are willing to enter upon a program of practicing the presence? Never doubt that it is a discipline.

It is the apparent simplicity or uncomplicatedness of such injunctions as to take no thought or to acknowledge God in *all* your ways that may cause you to ignore these instructions. If they are so simple, why do so few follow them and enjoy the fruitage of life lived consciously in the presence of God? Is it not because few can accept the omnipresence of God, continuing instead to seek some hard, difficult, and complicated method of attaining what they already are?

Make your New Year truly new by taking the principles in this letter and putting them into practice and thus enter into a whole new consciousness.

Chapter Two

From Practicing the Presence to the Prayer of Listening

L iving the spiritual life begins with practicing the presence of God, which means living in such a way that from the moment we awaken in the morning until we go to sleep at night, we have some conscious realization and acknowledgment of God. For example, on waking up in the morning, before jumping out of bed, wait for a few minutes and contemplate:

> This is a new day, which I had nothing to do with
> creating, nor had any man or woman. Where did it
> come from? Where, but from God? Therefore, this
> day must be the work of God, and if it is the work of
> God, it must include in it the works of God, the
> presence of God, and the power of God.

> I can begin with the activities of this day without
> worry and without fear because I know that since
> God has brought about this day, He will not leave it
> to its own resources. He created it and He maintains
> and sustains it. So I can safely trust this day to the
> government of God and to His presence and power.

Only after such a realization should we make our preparations for the day. At breakfast must come the realization that there could be no food on our table or on any table but for the grace of God. Only God can bring forth crops and fruits. We can plant the seeds, but we cannot make seeds and we cannot make them grow after they are planted. Some kind of a law must take hold of a seed in order to bring forth apples from apple seeds or peaches from peach seeds. Therefore it is by God's grace that the food we eat and drink is provided for us.

Meeting the Responsibilities of the Day

As we go forward during the day, there is not a person who is not faced with some responsibility greater than he is able to care for. No one of us goes through life without having problems that we cannot humanly solve, and it is in these periods that we again contemplate truth as we know it, remembering that "He performeth the thing that is appointed for me.[1] . . . The Lord will perfect that which concerneth me."[2] He that brought forth this day and will bring forth night after day performs that which is given us to do. The government is upon His shoulders.

As the day unfolds, with each problem that arises or even if it is not a problem but in the normal course of business, we find a freedom if, instead of believing that we alone are responsible, we remember that there is a He within us that is greater than any problem in the world. There is a He within us that gives us our ideas, strength, capital, experience, judgment, and wisdom.

Safety Through God-Realization

Most of us are aware of the dangers on the highways today stemming from traffic conditions, irresponsible drivers, and those who insist on driving while under the influence of alcohol. If we are merely trusting to luck or the law of averages to keep us out of trouble, sooner or later the average goes against us. Therefore, we should never get into an automobile, board a bus, a tram, or take any other form of transportation without the realization:

> God drives, He governs, and He controls.
> God is the mind of every individual and the intelli-
> gence. Safety and security are God's responsibility,
> and God is the love enfolding all.

Thus our safety is taken out of irresponsible or careless hands and placed where it belongs, in God's hands.

This is practicing the presence because we are consciously remembering, morning to night and night to morning, that we are not alone in this world and that we have more than human relatives and human friends: we have divine companionship; we have an inner grace. What we call It makes no difference at all—God, the spirit of God, or the Christ—as long as we recognize that It is divine in nature and that It has a function in our experience.

The kingdom of God is within. Is not Its function to go before us to "make the crooked places straight"³ and to create "mansions"⁴ for us? It is to go before us as protection and walk behind us as protection. What is to do this? The spirit of God, the presence of the Christ in us is to do this.

On my first trip to Australia, while I was giving a closed class in Melbourne, the voice spoke to me and said, "On your next flight you are going to meet trouble." I instantly stopped talking and said to the class, "I have just received a message that my next flight is going to bring trouble. So let us meditate until this thing is met." We meditated, and it took only a few minutes until an absolute assurance of God's presence came. Then we went on with the class.

My next flight was from Melbourne to Perth. We were about three-quarters of an hour out from Perth when one of the engines went out and we were floundering around with a dead engine. The pilot evidently sent for the stewardess who went to the rear of the plane and took up her position. Some of the passengers further back did not even notice that anything had happened, but I was sitting in the front part of the plane and saw the whole thing. Then the experience in the class and the assurance of God's presence came back to me. I just smiled as I thought, "Well, it will be interesting to see how it works out." Just about then the pilot made a couple of quick moves first in one direction and then in another, as if he were trying to force something. With that the engine sparked and came on. We were only twenty minutes late coming into Perth.

This same sort of thing happened some years ago when I was swimming in Honolulu and the voice said, "Soon you will be in trouble, but do not fear. *I* will be there." A few days later I had to go to the West Coast, took the plane, and we were just one hour out when I heard something amiss in the engine. The pilot did not make any move. When it happened a second time and the pilot made no move, I turned within and the voice said, "The next time he will move." The next time he did move and went back to Honolulu.

As we live this life, we make contact within, and always It goes before us to make the crooked places straight. It warns us of dangers ahead; It guides us in the direction of safety, harmony, and rightness. It becomes the cement of relationships between us and those we meet so that we do not have any really unpleasant experiences along the way. Most of the people we meet are very pleasant, and only rarely do we have an out-and-out unpleasant experience because the presence operates in all our relationships.

Great tragedies take place on earth every single day, and God does nothing to stop them. War takes place, with all its injustices, not only to adults but to the youngsters who are innocent victims of those conditions. Since we know this, we must understand that God does not function for us or for anyone else on earth unless we abide in the Word and know the truth consciously.

Scripture makes it very clear that "a thousand shall fall at [our] side, and ten thousand at [our] right hand; but it shall not come nigh [us]"[5] *if* we dwell "in the secret place of the most High."[6]

In the fifteenth chapter of John, Christ Jesus said that if we do not abide in this Word and if we do not let God abide in us, we will be as a branch of a tree that is cut off and withers. The withered branch is the human being who is having accidents, indulging in sin, and experiencing disease and tragedy, and we are of that ten thousand on the right unless we are consciously abiding in the Word and constantly acknowledging, "My grace is sufficient for thee."[7]

> Thy grace it is that supplies me.
> Thy grace is the health of my countenance. Thy grace
> is my protection. Thy grace goes before me.
> Thy grace feeds and sustains and
> clothes and houses me.

Are We Shutting God Out of Our Conscious Experience?

Unless we are living in this truth morning to night and night to morning, praying without ceasing, we are not abiding "in the secret place of the most High," and we become one of the thousand at the left or the ten thousand at the right.

It is up to each one of us to determine how much safety we want, how much security, how much prosperity, and how much health. Only we ourselves can determine this. When we discover that as the son and heir of God we are entitled to health, harmony, wholeness, completeness, protection, and abundant supply, then it is up to us. No one can give these things to us, not even God. Only we can bring them into our experience by consciously realizing:

> This is God's day, and it is His responsibility to gov-
> ern it. He is with me wherever I go, for He and I are
> one. In that oneness are found my safety, my security,
> my protection, my maintenance, and my sustenance.
> In my oneness with God I find my completeness.

If we are not rehearsing that morning, noon, and night, then we are shutting God out of our conscious experience. When the Prodigal Son wandered away and ended up in that feast with the swine, it was not that his father had left him: it was that he had left his father. The very moment he turned back, the father was there to greet him with the jeweled ring and the royal robe.

The Past Is Wiped Out in a Moment of Turning

"Though [our] sins be as scarlet,"[8] in one second we are "white as snow"[8] when we turn back to the Father, like Saul of Tarsus who experienced the revelation of the Christ in one blinding flash. From that moment on, his entire past was wiped out.

All of Moses' past was also wiped out when he had the vision of God on the Mount, and then instead of a wanderer and murderer set apart from his own country, he returned as the Hebrew leader and savior of that day.

Though our sins are scarlet, we become white as snow in any given instant. There need be no period of waiting. There is no period of waiting in outer halls or limbo. It is now! Now while we are on earth in our moment of turning within to the Christ and surrendering ourselves to the spirit of God, we are white as snow. Our sins, our diseases, and our poverty are removed because there is no time element in the spiritual life.

All of this can be brought into our experience in a moment, but by no one but us. A practitioner cannot do it for us, nor a teacher or a minister. Only we ourselves can determine that from waking up in the morning until retiring at night, and even waking up in the middle of the night, we will consciously remember to place the responsibility for the day and the night on the presence of God within us. "Greater is he that is in you, than he that is in the world."[9]

Practicing the Presence, the Preparation for Meditation

If we practice the presence of God for just a few months religiously and devotedly, automatically we are bringing about an inner stillness and quietness. We lose our fears of the outer world with its alarming newspaper headlines and epidemics because we have come to see that in the presence of God epidemics have no power. Where God is consciously realized, there is freedom from the sin, the disease, the lack, and the limitations of this world.

Inner quietness and stillness prepare us for the next experience, which is that of meditation. By having three periods every day of four, five, or six minute's duration, eventually, these periods stretch out to seven, eight, nine, or ten minutes. Then we are dissatisfied with only three in a day, and we squeeze in a fourth. Before long, we are apt to find that we are having ten, twelve, or fourteen of those periods, and they may be anywhere from two minutes to ten minutes each, but each one of them is a complete relaxing from personal selfhood and placing us in the position of hearing the still, small voice. This, of course, is the goal of the spiritual life: to live so that we receive impartations from God.

Christianity is a mystical religion because it includes the teaching that it is possible for us to receive answers to prayer, to hear the "still small voice,"[10] and to receive impartations from the Spirit. This is the goal of the Christian life. When we reach that goal, we will be able to say with Paul, "I live; yet not I, but Christ liveth in me."[11]

If we have something to take care of during the day, we close our eyes for a moment and instantly the guidance comes to us as to what to do or when, or whom to see. If we are composers and master the art of meditation, from the inner source melodies will flow such as man has never heard before. If we are in business and require new ideas, new inventions, or new designs, once we have achieved the ability to be still inwardly, these will flow into our experience, and we will be guided, led, directed, inspired, and protected. The stillness, the peace, and the assurance of God's presence that come to us through the practice of the presence of God now lead us into the second stage of deeper quiet, deeper stillness, until we do make contact and begin to receive impartations, directions, orders, wisdom, and light from within.

The Meaning of Prayer Without Words or Thoughts

Prayer is the major way of life on the spiritual path. It might be safe to say that prayer constitutes seventy-five percent of the day or night of a person who is living the spiritual life, and yet it does not require that he give up his home, business, or professional activities. He prays even while he is at work. Prayer on the spiritual path takes a different form from that to which a person has been accustomed in life.

To begin with, this form of prayer has in it no words and no thoughts in the sense that no words are ever addressed to God, no thoughts are ever sent to God, and no requests are ever made of God. Nothing is expected from God. This in itself changes entirely the nature of our prayer and makes it very easy to pray or to meditate.

I cannot remind students too often that God cannot be influenced. We cannot pray to God and make Him do our will or have Him give us our desires. That would be setting us up as greater than God and as having more wisdom or more love than God. If God is infinite intelligence, He needs no advice, no instructions from you or me, for He is the infinite, all-knowing

Consciousness, the Wisdom great enough to form this universe, to maintain it, to sustain it, and to give us the spiritual laws by which we live.

The great inventions we enjoy today were not invented by man. Man merely discovered the laws of God that govern them and then applied them. But even that had to be done under God's grace or it would not have been done.

How wonderfully are the stars, the sun, and the moon governed! God maintains and sustains the universe by spiritual law. Knowing that, to say to God, "I need rent," or "I need health," or "I need a companion," is insulting God. It is virtually saying, "God, I know my need more than You do, and I am telling it to You." No, on the spiritual path we accept God as infinite intelligence and divine love.

Praying Effectively

When we pray, we do not have to pray to God for anything. We merely have to pray within ourselves:

Thank You, Father, that You are the all-knowing, that
You are closer to me than breathing, and that it is
Your good pleasure to give me the Kingdom.

The thought may come, "But I did not pray for anything," and this is the great secret of true prayer.

Why are there so many billion prayers every week that are never answered? How many prayers ask for peace on earth, for food, for clothing, and for protection and are never answered? When we go to God for anything, we are asking God to be our servant and go out and get us something. We are asking God to be a messenger boy for us. "God, give me food." "God, give me clothing." "Here, Messenger Boy, run out and get this for me." There is no such God, and there are no such things to be given us by God.

God has only one gift to give, and that is the gift of Himself. Since God is infinite, there is not God *and* something else. God includes all else, and when we have God, we have all. When we do not have God, we have nothing. But let us never believe that we can go to God for some *thing*, because it cannot be done.

> Father, I am not coming to You for anything. I am resting in the assurance of Thy presence. Thy grace is my sufficiency. I seek nothing but Thee. If I can companion with Thee, if I can tabernacle with Thee, if I can rest in Thy presence, this is all I ask. Thy grace and Thy blessing are enough for me. I do not ask for anything for anybody. Instead I turn within and realize that Thou art "closer. . . than breathing, and nearer than hands and feet." Let Thy will be done on earth as it is in heaven. Thy grace is my sufficiency in all things.

Praying thus, we rest, turning within with an open ear as if we were expecting to hear the voice of God. We may not really hear a voice, but we may and sometimes we do, definitely and clearly.

Through inner listening and guidance, the Infinite Way activity has unfolded. The Christ is governing its activity and when It speaks, I follow. I do not inaugurate, I do not determine, nor do I pray to God and tell Him what I would like to have happen. I sit and wait with an expectant attitude, and in every detail the leading and the guidance and the protection come from within.

Living Out from an Inner Strength

I know from my experience and from that of our students that through meditation we come to a place where ultimately we receive protection, guidance, wisdom, and a strength far beyond what we humanly could know.

How persons who have not felt the touch of the Spirit limit themselves! Some persons who have had appointments with me frequently explain that they are not on time for their appointments because of their age, a fact they assumed I would surely understand. According to them, they were quite old, and of course it was not possible for them to keep up with everything the way they would like to. They talked so much about age that eventually I could not help saying, "You really do not look that old. How old are you?" and I discovered that one was a year younger than I and the other was two years older.

Is it not utter nonsense to believe that God creates us and then abandons us just because we reach a certain age? If we are without youth, strength, vitality, intelligence, and without our faculties, it is not because God has abandoned us: it is because we have abandoned God. Many men of ninety have continued to do the same amount of work they were doing at fifty. Many engaged in a spiritual work are in their eighties and nineties, and one would not believe it to look at them. They are functioning on a full day basis, too.

Once we have made the inner contact, we do not live only by the food we eat, what we drink, or by the air we breathe. We live by every word that proceeds out of the mouth of God. Every word that reveals itself within us is life to our body, to our mind, to our soul and spirit, and becomes the power of healing unto someone else.

Omnipotence Makes No Mistakes

We never ask God for healing for ourselves or for anyone else, nor do we ever tell God that our patient has rheumatism or some other ailment. We do not carry any burdens up to God. We drop the burdens, turn within, and let the Father reveal His presence to us. As that Presence is revealed, something happens in the consciousness of the patient. But this can come only when we understand the principle that God does not heal disease, God never has healed disease, and God never will heal disease.

The secret of spiritual healing is that since God is infinite and omnipotent, nothing but God has power, and therefore, the sin, the disease, the belief, or the claim is without power. We do not expect God to heal disease because God is already infinite, God is already maintaining His spiritual creation, and we come under the healing law in proportion as we realize God's omnipotence.

We cannot say in one breath, "Oh, yes, God is almighty, God is all-power," and then add, "but this little flu germ is annoying me." That will not do. We cannot claim God's omnipotence and then believe that there is power in germs, weather, climate, or age. We either have God as omnipotence or we might as well leave God out. We can prove God's omnipotence the moment we stop trying to get God to do something. All that God is doing, God is doing now. God is the same yesterday, today, and forever, and God cannot start today to do something. God cannot correct something, because God has made no mistakes.

Recognizing the Non-power of Discord

God has no knowledge whatever of the sin, disease, or lack we are carrying around, for He is too pure to behold iniquity. Therefore, it has no existence or power. It has existence only through the universal acceptance of two powers. There are discords on earth, not because of a devil because there is no devil. The devil is just a term manufactured to frighten us. But there is no devil, none whatsoever. There is a universal belief that there are two powers, which according to scripture came from the allegory of Adam and Eve who accepted good and evil. Up to that moment there was no evil: no sin, no disease, no death, no pain. But we are told that because Adam and Eve accepted two powers, a good power and an evil power, they were cast out of Eden.

We are the Adam and Eve cast out of Eden. Right now we

are accepting a good power and an evil power, but the omnipotence of God makes it impossible for there to be an evil power. Therefore, all the evil that exists, exists in our minds. The world accepts certain germs as the cause of certain diseases, but every metaphysical healing is a proof that those germs are not evil powers because without doing anything to the germs, the disease is healed. How is the disease healed? We do not touch the germs; we do not prescribe anything to get rid of them. We sit in the silence and realize, "God is omnipotent, and therefore nothing else is power." Living out from that consciousness, very soon we hear from the patient that he is better, and usually it is not long until he is healed.

Whatever healings take place through metaphysical or spiritual means take place because of a practitioner's realization of the omnipotence of God and the non-power of what is claiming to be sin, disease, lack, or limitation.

Opening the Circuit Within

When we receive impartations, we begin to understand what Christ Jesus meant when he said, "I will never leave thee, nor forsake thee.[12]. . . It is I; be not afraid.[13]. . . Before Abraham was, I am.[14]. . . I am with you always, even unto the end of the world.[15]. . . I am the way, the truth, and the life."[16] Ah, but what about all these germs? What about all these years of the calendar that have gone over my head? When such temptations come, we turn in meditation and again we hear, "Fear not! *I* am with you. *I* will never leave you." What does this mean, if it does not mean that we are under divine protection, divine care, divine healing, divine love, eternal immortal life?

When we enter the mystical, the spiritual, or contemplative way of life, we take as our model of prayer these passages in Luke: "Take no thought for your life, what ye shall eat; neither for the body, what ye shall put on. . . . Your Father knoweth that ye have need of these things. . . . It is your Father's good pleasure to give you the kingdom."[17] Having prayed thus, we turn within and realize:

> I am not coming to You for anything. I am not asking for anything, nor am I trying to tell You what things I have need of. I am coming here only to rest in the assurance of Your presence and grace.

> Reveal Yourself to me. Let me feel Your presence. I have wandered so far away from Your house. I have been away from You so long in thought. Let me return and find my home in You.

> I will be satisfied with Your grace. I will be satisfied with Your will for me. I will be satisfied with Your plan. You know my need, and it is Your good pleasure to give me the kingdom. And now, I have said enough. Speak, Lord, it is Your turn. Your servant is listening.

Then we open the ear for only a minute or two. That is all that is necessary, and we pay no attention at all to the fact that we may not hear or feel anything. That makes no difference. After a minute or two or three, we get up and go about our work. If there is any need for us to hear anything or to be instructed or led, it will take place at the time when it is necessary. There is no such thing even as telling God when we want Him to talk to us. We merely tune in, and then rest assured that when the time comes for receiving guidance, it will be there.

If we practice this kind of meditation three, four, or five times a day, eventually, we will have opened a circuit within ourselves, a place of contact. It is as if we have created a vacuum, and into that the Spirit eventually flows. No longer will we waste precious years asking God for something when there is but one thing God can give us, and that is Himself.

Seek God Alone

When we have the spirit of God dwelling in us, all things are added unto us, but we cannot seek *things* in prayer. We can seek only His presence, His grace.

Let us try to imagine Spirit filling all space, infinite space. Can anything else be added to that Infinity? There is no room for food, clothing, and housing outside of Infinity, so that whatever is necessary, we get when we have God, the Infinite Invisible.

What we are really seeking is a divine gift, but God has no gift to give because there is not Infinity and something else to give: there is only Infinity Itself, there is only spiritual Being Itself, and that is God. When the spirit of God dwells in us, we are free and we have all. We are heir of God to all the heavenly riches without asking for anything. Being joint-heirs entitles us to all that God has.

When we are not going to God to get something or to use God for any purpose, it is very easy to settle down into meditation and realize:

What a joy it is to be in Thy presence.
I come to Thee, Father, as I would visit my own
mother, not seeking something, but just for companionship, for the renewal of an assurance of Thy presence and Thy grace. I have food and clothing and
housing, and once I have Thy grace I have health,
immortality, youth, strength, power.
Once I have Thy grace I have protection.

Anyone can come into the spiritual way of life if he is prepared to give up asking, demanding, or expecting something of God, and if he turns his whole heart and soul to seeking the realization of God, the feeling or the awareness of God's presence. Having attained that, he can watch how God's grace does all the rest.

This makes it possible to follow Paul in his statement: "I live; yet not I, but Christ liveth my life." The Christ is going before us. The Christ is protecting, the Christ is sustaining, the Christ is supplying, the Christ is feeding.

We can picture the barrier to our good that is set up when we believe we are going to God over there to get something for us over here. Let us cut out this person over here entirely and the something that he thinks he wants and go directly to the God within. When we do, the two will come together and they will find that they are not two any more: they are one. "I and my Father are one."[18] Right now, it may appear that I and the Father are two, that I am a human being here and there is a God up there, in here, outside, or somewhere. But in meditation the two come together, and then we find that the Father is within us, and we are one, not two. With that, this passage of scripture really comes alive: "Son, thou art ever with me, and all that I have is thine." [19] That becomes one of the greatest prayers that we can carry in our consciousness.

"Son,"—that is the Father speaking to us from within— "Son, thou art ever with me, and all that I have is thine." In that, we relax. We do not ask for anything and we do not pray for anything: we merely believe that all that the Father has is ours. In relaxing in that, it will not be long until God's grace is flowing to us in such measure that it will be pressed down and running over, all because we have learned not to ask for things, but desire only to know Him, whom to know aright is life eternal.

ACROSS THE DESK

Since *The Gift of Love* has been released to the world, it cannot help but uplift humanity. It is simple and inspiring, touching the heart and releasing it of its burdens. Let us take *The Gift of Love* into consciousness and live with it day by day and hour by hour.

As we work with the message in this book, we, too, will be

building that consciousness of love which is the healing and redeeming consciousness.

TAPE RECORDED EXCERPTS
Prepared by the Editor

"When we keep our mind stayed on God throughout the day and night, when we acknowledge God as the health of our countenance, as our safety and security, as our all, it is only a very few days until we find ourselves in an inner peace, at least more peace than before, and perhaps even a greater assurance. . . . We have acknowledged so often the reality of God in our human experience that it comes back to us from within us with this assurance: 'You are right, *I Am* with you. *I* do go before you.'

"We receive some kind of an assurance that stops a great deal of our anxious thought because now we are entertaining God consciously within us. It is an impossibility to walk up and down the world with God consciously with us, and then fear, doubt, or hate.

"Now when we sit down, the mind is not as rambunctious as it was before. It is more subject unto us, so that when we sit down and commence to contemplate God's grace, God's availability, God's presence, it only takes a very few moments of that contemplation until inwardly thought really quiets down. Sometimes it is only for a couple of seconds, but that couple of seconds can be recaptured several times a day. As we continue both practicing the presence and meditation, eventually this inner peace will remain with us for as much as a minute. It doesn't have to be a minute: one second is enough to transform anyone's life."

Joel S. Goldsmith, "The Peak of Mystical Living," *The 1960 New York Closed Class.*

Chapter Three

Meditation, the Door to Fulfillment

There is a way of preventing most of the world's discords from acting upon you. That way is through meditation. It is through meditation that you come into a conscious awareness of the dominion given you in the beginning. A meditation to establish yourself in the consciousness of oneness is an important step:

> The law of God operates in me, in my mind and in
> my body. I am subject only to that law flowing out
> from within. From the kingdom of God within me, I
> receive divine impartations which, through my mind,
> govern my body, my home, and my business.

> I have a body, and this body is mine.
> I have control over it. I control my hands so that they
> cannot steal and my feet so they cannot run away.
> The body does not control itself, but I control this
> body, and it is responsive to my will.

> I also have a mind, and I do not permit that
> mind to think thoughts that come to it from the

external world. I have as much control over my
mind as I have over my body, so I use my mind to
think my own thoughts. I cannot waste energy letting
my mind wander into idle subjects, for the mind is
an instrument, and it must be kept in as good
condition as the body. Therefore, just as I do not
turn my body over to anyone else, neither do I turn
my mind over to anyone else, nor do I turn my
body or my mind over to the world at large.

God gave me this mind and this body, and I have
God-given dominion over mind and body, so that
nothing can in any wise enter my mind to violate my
integrity, to cause distress, sin, disease, death, or
limitation. I am always back of me,
thinking My thoughts through my mind, and
governing my body through my mind. I do not
deliver my mind to another to work upon.

Becoming Free of Universal Malpractice

There is a silent universal mind action, mesmerism, hypnotism, or malpractice which uses the mind of an individual
to inform him that there is infection, contagion, unemployment, a depression, or bad weather. But now let us take this
mind and realize:

This is my mind, a God-given mind,
given to me for my use and not the world's use.
Therefore, I am not subject to world beliefs
or world thoughts. I am not subject to the ambitions,
lusts, or malpractice of the world. I am not subject to
the ignorance or fears of the world, for I and the
Father are one, and all that the Father has is mine.
I receive my guidance, my direction, my life,

and my law from God. The will of God
is done in me, in my mind and in my body.

My home, my business, my profession, these are all
encompassed within me, and they are not subject to
world belief or world malpractice. They are not
subject to "man, whose breath is in his nostrils,"[1]
for they are embodied within me, and I have
God-given jurisdiction over mind and body, and over
my concepts of home, family, business, profession,
or whatever my interests may be.

I am not acted upon by outside influences. The kingdom of God flows out from within me and acts as a
law of good unto my mind and body and business,
unto my home and health, and unto my profession.

I do not lend my mind or body to any outside
malpractice, to any outside beliefs of a
universal or personal nature. "I and my Father are
one,"[2] and all that the Father has is mine.
The place whereon I stand is holy ground.

All jurisdiction comes from God and flows through
me, unto my world and my affairs. God is the
governing agent, leading, directing, guiding, feeding,
sustaining, maintaining, and all from within me.

Because the above meditation is a conscious activity of your
consciousness, it becomes the law unto you. The world mesmerism is so great, however, that you will undoubtedly feel the
need to meditate not only in the morning but in the afternoon
and at night. You will not, of course, repeat any particular meditation or form of meditation, but each day you will meditate on
whatever subject comes to you.

The Principle of Fulfilling Relationships

One of the most important subjects that will ever come up in your spiritual life is that of human relationships: relationships with your family, your community, your business, and the world. The chapters, "Love Thy Neighbor" in *Practicing the Presence,*[3] and "Relationship of Oneness," in *The Art of Spiritual Healing,*[4] present specific principles in regard to such relationships. They point out that since there is but one infinite, divine self, one life, one mind, one being, the *I* or Selfhood of you is the *I* or Selfhood of every member of your family, every person in your business, and every member of your community. What you do to one of them you do to yourself. All conduct has to be based on that. Any injustice you do to another is done to you, for there is but one *I,* one divine Self.

The love you express is being expressed to you. It might seem that you are expressing it to another person, but in the end it is coming back to you because there is a spiritual law which says, "Cast thy bread upon the waters: for thou shalt find it after many days."[5] And why does it say that? Because no bread can come back to you except what you, yourself, cast on the waters. Every scrap that is on the waters was put there by someone, and it is earmarked for return to him. You can only get your fingers burned trying to get somebody else's bread. "Cast your bread upon the waters," and you will find that that which you send forth to another is that which rebounds to you.

Whatsoever a man soweth,
that shall he also reap.

For he that soweth to his flesh shall of the flesh reap
corruption; but he that soweth to the Spirit shall of
the Spirit reap life everlasting.

Galatians 6:7,8

Whatever law you accept becomes the law unto you. If you sow to the flesh, if you sow for gain at somebody else's expense, if you sow to injustice, if you sow to slander and scandalmongering, that is what you will reap. If you cheat, steal from, or defraud another, which is certainly sowing to the flesh, that is what must inevitably return to you. But if you sow to the Spirit, if you permit love, justice, mercy, benevolence, and forgiveness to flow out from you, you reap life everlasting. It is the karmic law of ancient scripture.

The bread that you cast on the waters returns to you. That is why you have to be careful not to send forth stale bread. Had we accepted the teaching of Jesus Christ on this score literally, we would have known hundreds of years ago that we dig our own graves by our conduct, by the atmosphere we carry with us, and by our attitude to others. What you do to others is the measure that returns to you pressed down and running over.

You can think of it this way: the *I* of me is the *I* of you. When I take money from my pocket and give it to you, it is just as if I took it out of my right-hand pocket and put it into my left-hand pocket. It is earmarked for return, and usually with interest. The forgiveness that I give to another, I am giving to myself, and quickly it will return to me. That to which I hold another in bondage is eventually that to which I, myself, am held in bondage. It must inevitably be, for there is but one *I;* there is but one Ego; there is but one Selfhood, and the Selfhood of me is the Selfhood of you.

Responsibility for Individual and National Acts

Nations do not understand that the cumulative acts of all their citizens together decide the ultimate fate of the nation. There are those who think that nations can engage in war and achieve a victory. They believe that it is possible to go to war and not be required to pay back every bit that they have handed out. Those who have had the wisdom to learn the lesson of war must certainly be aware of what has happened to all those involved in war, whether their nation was on what was presumably the right side or the wrong side. The truth is that there is no right side to any war.

Even if we are not wholly responsible for the acts of our government, to some extent we all share that responsibility because we participate in the benefits that seem to accrue from those acts. For our purpose at this present time, however, we will deal only with our individual acts and conduct within our family, business, and community circle. We must remember to live as if what we are doing to another we are doing to ourselves. If we do not keep that in mind, sooner or later we will be led astray into thinking that we can benefit at another's expense. And so it goes in an endless circle. It is wise to have a few minutes of meditation on this subject at least once a day:

> There is only one infinite Life.
> My life is your life, and therefore what I do to your
> life, I do to my own. There is only one spiritual Soul,
> infinite, eternal, and immortal. Whatever I do to
> your soul, I do to my own.

Such a meditation will begin to change your whole outlook towards the world, because now you can no longer compartmentalize people into Jew or Greek, bond or free, black or white. Now it becomes evident that underneath the skin, or in that kingdom of God within, all are one in spiritual sonship, all branches of the same vine. Anything then that affects one branch eventually will affect all branches.

Gaining the Awareness of Supply As Universally Available

Another time your meditation may take you to the subject of supply. There is no one so rich that he does not need lessons on supply just as much as those who have nothing. Supply does not have to do with how many dollars a person has. As a matter of fact how many dollars he has tonight has no relationship to the number of dollars he may have a week from tonight. Supply must be considered from an entirely different standpoint than that of dollars, plus or minus. As you meditate on the subject of supply, the first thought that may come to mind is:

"The earth is the Lord's, and the fulness thereof." [6]
There is only one supply. Anything I do to your
supply, I do to my supply.

"Son, thou art ever with me, and all that I have is
thine." [7] In this minute I surrender the personal sense
of possession and realize that whatever
I have has come forth from God,
and I am willing that it be returned to God.

"The earth is the Lord's, and the fulness thereof." That includes the trees, the mines, the oceans, the pearls, the diamonds, the gold, the crops, the fruits, the berries. Before there was a human being on earth and if there should ever be a time with no human beings on earth, it would still be true that "the earth is the Lord's, and the fulness thereof." Any deed or claim that anyone may have to a part of it is just a temporary arrangement.

The Bread of Life

Jesus did not try to turn stones into bread because he knew that it was God's function to feed him. So it is with us. It is not our function to take thought: it is God's function.

"Man shall not live by bread alone, but by every word that proceedeth out of the mouth of God." [8] Supply is the word of God; supply is every word of truth that comes from the kingdom of God within. Every word of truth that we entertain in consciousness, every word of truth we abide in or that we permit to abide in us, this is our supply.

Since God is spirit, all of God's creation must be spiritual, and supply therefore must be spiritual. That is why we do not live by bread alone, but by every word that proceeds out of the mouth of God.

"He that abideth in me, and I in him, the same bringeth forth much fruit."[9] What difference does it make whether Jesus said bread, or fruit, or meat? It is all the same thing. It means substance. It means supply. The Master never said that supply is money or property. He said, "I am the bread of life."[10] In other words, *I* is supply, *I* is all forms of supply.

Because supply is spiritual and always omnipresent, we already have it in infinite abundance. When we say *I*, we are declaring the source of bread, meat, wine, water, resurrection, and life eternal. *I* in the midst of us is supply. *I* in the midst of us is our bread, meat, wine, water. Now we do not have to take thought for supply. We do not have to earn our supply by the sweat of our brow. Rather do we go out to our daily work for the joy of service, for the joy of the work itself. Our supply is dependent on our understanding of the truth that *I Am* is supply. We embody supply. We include within us the substance of life. Within that *I,* which is our own being, within that *I* within us is all that we have been seeking out in the world.

Work, Not for a Living, But for the Joy of Serving

With this assurance we can go out into the world, thinking only of how well we can do the job, of how many ways we can serve and be useful, whether to our employer or the public, of how many ways we can bless.

If we can do nothing else, we can bring with us the power of forgiveness, so that wherever we see sin, disease, or death, we do not condemn but forgive. If we can do nothing else in our work, we can be a benediction at every step, by realizing, "God is with you. Immanuel, peace be unto this household. Peace be unto this business office. Peace be unto this customer. Peace be unto this client."

Since supply is spiritual, we can give everybody an infinity of supply: a supply of life, gratitude, forgiveness, commendation, and a supply of peace on earth. Because we are the sons of God, we are heirs of God, heirs to all the heavenly riches. That is why we do not work merely for a living but for the service we can give. *I* within us is the son of God, and It is the source of all supply. So now we are free to go out to bless, to give, and to serve.

"Except the Lord Keep the City"

There are times when, because of the news of the day, the thought of danger is in the air, and this brings us to a consideration of the subject of safety and security.

> "Except the Lord build the house, they labor in vain
> that build it." [11] Except the Lord be my protection, it
> would be a waste of time for me to try to protect
> myself from all the germs, bullets, accidents,
> automobiles, and airplanes in the world.

> The presence of God is my security. Except the Lord
> build a sure defense round about me, it would be
> foolish for me to try to defend myself from the evils
> of the world. "Except the Lord build the house," I
> would labor in vain. "Except the Lord keep the city,
> the watchman waketh but in vain." [11] But the Lord is
> keeping the watch, and all is well.

Spontaneous Unfoldment, Not Memorized Statements

The word of God comes up spontaneously within us, so we need never concern ourselves with what we are going to think, or even with what truth we are going to use in treatment or meditation. As we read Infinite Way books and hear the tape recordings, enough truth will be planting itself in our consciousness, so that when there is a need for truth, something will come forth to meet that need.

From day to day as we have our meditations, different themes for meditation will come to us, and each time the meditation may be different. We do not memorize anything. In fact, trying to memorize truth could be very harmful because depending on something we remember would be depending on a broken reed. No, we depend on God. Our memory is not God. Our meditations must be spontaneous and original each time we turn within.

We do not live on yesterday's manna. That is a principle applicable to supply, whether the supply is of dollars or healing meditations. God's manna falls as we need it, and we never have to gather enough to last until tomorrow. We do not have to remember any statements of truth for tomorrow, nor do we have to fill our heads with memorized statements of truth because they will be of no value. All they will be is a lot of words and thoughts, and these can never be God.

When we have a healing contemplative meditation or give a treatment, we do not try to use the same meditation or treatment that healed a serious disease yesterday, because today it may not heal a cold or a headache. We never try to memorize a treatment that brought somebody employment today because tomorrow it may not bring him a farthing. But as we turn to the Father within, to that infinite storehouse, what comes through spontaneously is the word of God. The word of God is quick and sharp and when He utters His voice, the earth melts. It is only the spontaneity of God that can meet our need.

If we could recite all the truth that is in the Bible and all metaphysical writings, that would not be God uttering His voice. That would just be a parroting of words, and there is no spiritual power in such statements of truth. It has to be the word of God that God utters, not your word or mine. So if we are going to give a treatment or have a healing meditation, we sit down, close our eyes, and turn to the Father within in a listening attitude.

We may give a treatment using whatever truth we know, but we cannot stop there and feel that the treatment is complete. That is only the preparation for the treatment which takes place when we have finished with our particular voicing of truth, and say, "Speak, Lord; I've had my say. Now You have Yours."

Then we listen, are still, and wait for something to come through from within. It does not have to be a message. It can be just a deep breath, a feeling of release, or like a weight dropping from the shoulders. It matters not how it comes, but when it comes we will know of a certainty that He has uttered His voice, and the error will melt. Sometimes it melts instantaneously; sometimes it seems to take longer, and we may have to repeat the treatment or meditation. But even if we have to work for a year to see through a problem, the object always is to let our treatment carry us as far as it will, and then wait for God to utter His voice. His word is strong and powerful and instantaneous.

The Activity of Grace

That brings us to the subject of Grace. Grace comes as a spontaneous gift or activity of God, not because we have earned it, not because we are worthy or deserving of it. It is what Paul described when he said, "I live; yet not I, but Christ liveth in me,"[12] meaning that we merely carry out here on the outer plane what God gives us to do.

If we have a task to do and it is done better than we could have done it, more promptly, quickly, or more profitably, we know that there must be an agency operating above and beyond our human intelligence or human strength.

When we begin to realize and understand the activity of Grace in our business, business begins to come to us that we ourselves made no human effort to get, and it comes in greater volume than we had thought possible. Sometimes ideas seem to come out of nowhere. Then we begin to understand the nature of Grace.

Grace takes place when we prepare for it. If we devote our energies to seeking to know God aright, eventually we not only come to know Him aright, but we find that all things have been added to us. We were not thinking about the things; we were not thinking about the demonstration; we were not thinking about places and persons. Our whole mind was stayed on God. The things were added because the moment we came into the Presence, we found that "in thy presence is fulness of joy."[13] The minute we attain the Presence, the fulness is there.

God Has Only Itself To Give

Only as we seek and attain the consciousness of the presence of God does the Presence go before us and draw all things to us. There is no way, really, of using God to attain our purpose, whether it is home, companionship, or supply; and we lose the demonstration of Grace when we think, "Here am I, and there is God, and here is my demonstration."

If we think we can go to God for things, we have not even started in the kindergarten of a spiritual teaching, because there is no "me" *and* God. There is no God *and* supply or God *and* companionship or God *and* safety. Such things exist only in fiction, an idea that began in pagan days and has been perpetuated. We cannot go to God, for I and the Father are already one, right here. So there is no place to go, and there is no one to whom to go. All that *I*, God, am, is already included here within us.

Since God is the substance of all creation, God made all that was made, and all that God made is good. God and His creation are one. We cannot go to God to get something *here*, and we cannot even go outside ourselves to find God, for God *is* our

Self. Moses' revelation, "I Am That I Am,"[14] would have shocked the world, so he quickly told his brother not to go down and tell the people because they would never have believed it. Moses knew that at that stage of their development they would believe only what their eyes could see, so he could not tell them. For centuries and centuries only the high priests of the Hebrew faith were allowed to know the name of God, and never under any conditions were they allowed to voice it except when they were inside that sanctuary with the holy Ark.

Jesus was crucified because he decided to tell the truth to the people. For the first time since Moses he told them, "*I* am He. *I*, the Father within you, am He. My Father and your Father is within you, not in holy mountains or holy temples to be worshiped, but within *you*."

Every mystic who has ever lived, from ancient records up to this present time, has received the same revelation: *I*, the one Ego, the one omnipresent Consciousness. In fact, one of the great English mystical poets was able to state, "Before God was, I am," meaning that before there were any fairy tales about a Santa Claus-God that rewards us when we are good and punishes us when we are bad, *I Am*.

ACROSS THE DESK

"Where the spirit of the Lord is, there is liberty." That liberty and freedom come to every student who seriously practices Infinite Way principles. The practice lies in reinterpreting world pictures, whether good or bad, well or sick, rich or poor. The great danger to students on the way, however, is to become satisfied merely with pleasant humanhood, and therefore, the importance of seeing through the good appearance cannot be pointed out too often.

As the student's awareness deepens, greater and greater demands are made upon his realized spiritual consciousness, demands from which no student should shrink. He cannot avoid accepting the responsibility for his own spiritual progress which frequently is in direct ratio to his conscious effort to reinterpret the human picture.

The impact of such reinterpretation upon his human life is boundless. Those who come into contact with a student seriously working with this principle cannot help but feel the Presence if any degree of receptivity has been attained.

Tape Recorded Excerpts
Prepared by the Editor

There are many names for error, all of them for the express purpose of revealing its nature as nothingness. One term that registers with many student and helps them better to understand this baffling problem is the use of the word "fabric." What is the fabric of which the world is made, that fabric we see with our eyes and are aware of through the physical senses? What is its substance? Is it what we see as conditions, persons, and things? The following excerpts will give you a much clearer realization of the nature of this world.

"The Fabric of Nothingness"

"All forms of error—whether appearing to you as forms of disease, forms of sin, forms of accident, forms of lack or limitation, forms of bad weather—are but forms of the one evil, the one error which is a universal hypnotism or the carnal mind. . . . In our work we do not handle rheumatism as a physical disease, nor do we handle a mental cause for a physical disease. We go right back to the fabric of which all forms of disease or lack or wars are made: the fabric of nothingness. It is the fabric called 'carnal mind,' 'appearance,' 'mesmerism,' 'hypnotism,' any name you wish to give to nothingness.

"When you abide constantly in the realization of God as the only power, you develop a consciousness. . . through study and practice which does not honor any form of evil but which instantly is realized as nothingness, as that which has no entity or identity as actual creation, but exists only as a mental form, a mental image without substance.

"Suppose I were to close my eyes and visualize or build in my mind a street, . . . a street that has on it some brick houses, a redwood house, and a house of hollow tiles. On this street there is green grass, and there are pink roses, glass windowpanes, and children playing. When I open my eyes, where is my street? I find that it never had existed at all. It existed as a mental image in thought without substance, except the substance of imagination. And it is gone.

"The young student says, 'But not my disease. That doesn't disappear so quickly.' Indeed it does not until your disease is brought to the consciousness of Jesus Christ. Then watch how quickly it disappears. . . . Why? Because in the consciousness of Jesus Christ, error had no power. . . . All his healings were brought out through his realization that God constitutes your being. 'Call no man on earth your father, for one is your Father which is in heaven'—which is within you. 'The Father within you, he doeth the works.' This is your Father, the infinite divine Life, the immortal Truth, . . . and you are the son."

Joel S. Goldsmith, "The Fabric of Nothingness,"
The 1958 New York Closed Class.

"Suppose you were dreaming that you are out in the water. As you look around, you find that you've gone out too far and you can't get back. Now begins your struggle to get back. There you are out in the water struggling. Is there a you? Is there water? Is there a struggle? No! What is the fabric or substance of the struggle? Your dream. The dream is the substance, and you, the water, and the struggle are the objects which are formed by your dream.

"If we were to take a leather cover and make a man here, a piano here, and a sky over there, we would still have neither man, piano, nor sky: we would have leather. In the destruction of the leather, there would be the destruction of the man, the piano, and the sky. In the destruction of your dream, there was the destruction of the you in the water, the water, and the struggle.

"The fabric of the discords of human experience is a universal hypnotism, a universal belief. . . . That is the fabric of every sense of limitation that can come into your experience, whether it is limited finances, limited health, limited family relations, or limited discordant business experience. The fabric of it is a universal hypnotism, a universal belief of a universe apart from God. . . .

"Always the realization that you are dealing with a fabric, not the picture that the fabric presents but the fabric itself, is your saving grace. In other words, we never have a dying person or a diseased person. We have a state of universal hypnotism appearing as a sick, sinful, dying, or dead person. We never have a bad person: we have a state of universal ignorance appearing as a bad person. The moment we realize that, the bad person disappears, and the fabric along with it. Then we are enabled to behold him as he really is.

"We have no dying person: we have an illusory sense of death. When we handle that, the dying person jumps up and says, 'Here I am, all new and fresh,' because you haven't done anything to a dying person who didn't exist to begin with. You have destroyed the fabric of the appearance. . . . There is no other way of overcoming the world."

Joel S. Goldsmith, "The Secret of Healing,"
The First Kailua Study Group.

"All sin, all disease, all lack, all limitation, and all wars are forms of material sense. When you destroy material sense you have no substance out of which those forms can appear. That is the spiritual secret. That is the secret of spiritual healing. That is the secret of spiritual living. . . . What is the nature of error? Material sense appearing as form.

"There is no use trying to get rid of the form. Don't try to get rid of sin or sinners; don't try to get rid of disease; don't try to get rid of lack or limitation. Those are only the decoys. Those are the forms which error assumes. But error is material sense, and the only thing that dissolves material sense is spiritual consciousness, the voice, the divine presence. . . .When you have God in action in your consciousness, material sense is dissolved, and when it is dissolved its forms disappear.

"You have seen in restaurant windows great big pieces of ice formed as birds, as eagles, as rocks, great big pieces of ice carved into wonderful forms of fish or animals. What happens when the ice melts? All the animals and fish disappear. So it is that all evil is nothing more nor less than a block of ice called material sense, and nothing is going to dissolve it except the Voice, except the presence of God. . . except the realization of God's presence. When you have that, material sense is dissolved, and when that is dissolved, false appetites disappear, false desires disappear, homelessness disappears, lack and limitation disappear, even wars disappear. . . . Material sense can be dissolved only by an individuals attaining God-realization."

Joel S. Goldsmith, "God-Realization Dissolves Material Sense," *The 1956 Second Steinway Hall Closed Class.*

Chapter Four

The Stature of
Spiritual Manhood

The original unfoldment or revelation given to me was that God is not in the human scene until God is admitted into our consciousness. In other words, all the evils that exist—individual, collective, national, and international—all these are possible because a human being as a branch of the Tree of Life is cut off and withers and dies.

As human beings we are separate and apart from God. We are that "natural man"[1] who knows not the things of God and cannot know them for they must be spiritually discerned. The things of God cannot be known with the mind; they cannot be known with the intellect; and this accounts for a great deal of the failure that many students experience in metaphysical work. Where there is failure, the reason is nearly always the same. It is not because of the particular message: it is that the individual is depending entirely on what he reads, on statements of truth and books, on hymns, or on church attendance, and none of these is God. None of these is spiritual power. The books, the teachers, and the churches, holy mountains, holy temples, and holy scriptures have their place, but they serve only as instruments whereby students develop the capacity of spiritual discernment.

Spiritual Discernment Is Essential

If the things of God could be known through the mind, everybody could read spiritual books and have access to God, but these do not provide that access. Access to God is attained only through spiritual discernment, and therefore, God does not enter your life or mine until we have developed some measure of spiritual discernment.

True, just as the Master could heal, feed, and forgive, so today those of spiritual discernment can do some measure of healing work, some feeding and forgiving, and some breaking of bondage to karmic law. But that is only of temporary help. To be rid of one disease does not mean that a person will not have another one. To experience a demonstration of supply does not mean that a person will not lack again. He probably will until the time comes when spiritual discernment is awakened in him. Then he finds that all the errors of mortal sense gradually begin to recede and to lessen in his experience.

That no one in his earthly experience will avoid one hundred per cent of these errors is indicated both in the experience of the Master, of Paul, and of present-day teachers. We have no record of any spiritual teacher of today being completely lifted above the discords of this world, but certainly problems of any name and nature come to him in an ever lessening degree.

The purpose of the message of the Infinite Way is to develop our spiritual faculties so that through these faculties we may discern God and the things of God and receive the grace of God, the peace of God, and the benediction of God.

When this was first revealed to me, the next question that arose was: How is this accomplished? How does one teach another to develop the spiritual faculty of discernment and the ability to receive God's grace? Eventually the answer that was given to me was that it comes through meditation.

Begin by Practicing the Presence

Meditation is not simple for those who have never approached it. It is made easier, however, by beginning not with meditation itself but with practicing the presence of God. It means consciously remembering God, acknowledging Him in all our ways, and remembering upon waking in the morning:

> Today I watch the activity of God
> taking place throughout the day.
> I will not fear what mortal man or mortal
> circumstances can do to me, but I will live as a
> beholder of God as God reveals each unfolding
> minute to me, each unfolding five minutes and each
> unfolding ten minutes, until at the end of the day I
> will be able to report, "God, You have done a
> wonderful job with today. I'm going to rest and
> trust You with the night."

In practicing the presence of God, we turn over the days and the nights to God. Eventually we turn over our household, our finances, our business, and the driving of our automobiles to God, even the driving of other drivers. Yes, we even place them under God's grace. Gradually by this practice of the Presence, it becomes a simple matter to meditate because now, as we sit down, we automatically find ourselves in the midst of an inner quiet and an inner rhythm.

To help us begin this practice, there is *Practicing the Presence*.[2] Then *The Art of Meditation*[3] takes us further and deeper into meditation. In *The World Is New*[4] we discover what happens when, through practicing the presence of God and meditation, the Presence enters our consciousness and begins to live our life for us.

We Limit Our Infinite Capacities
for Living by Finite Concepts

Our Spiritual Resources[5] reveals that each one of us has within himself an infinite capacity for life and for living, not a capacity that is limited by education, environment, nationality, or religion, but actually an infinite capacity for life, for joy, for income, and for outgo, a capacity that is not limited to our human capacity. Through spiritual discernment, we become aware of our spiritual resources, those resources which God placed in us in the beginning before ever the world was.

Jesus' prayer was, "O Father, glorify thou me with thine own self with the glory which I had with thee before the world was."[6] That glory is made up of the infinite nature of God, of Its qualities and capacities, and these constitute the glory we had in the beginning before this world was, this world of limited, finite concepts, in fact, before God was, that is, before the limited, finite concepts of God with which we have been brought up.

Our lives are limited primarily because we have a limited concept of man. In the human experience we believe that we watch man develop, grow, and disintegrate from the cradle to the grave. As we look at infants, children, youth, the mature, and the aged, we may think that these stages constitute man, and then it is no wonder we are so limited, if we are. But this that we behold is not man. This is the finite concept of man that came into existence when we accepted a selfhood apart from God.

Living in the Garden-of-Eden-Consciousness

There was a time when we knew that God, the Father, and God, the son, were one, when we actually lived the life of "I and my Father are one."[7] When we lived in the realization that *I* in the midst of us is our bread, meat, wine, and water, we lived consciously in the realization, "I have hidden manna, I have meat the world knows not of." Living in that consciousness, there was no concern, no fear, no doubt, no worry, no anxiety, and therefore, no frayed nerves and no old age. Of course, there was no disease and there was no death because no one can ever die, and no one can really be diseased once he has come to this realization:

> I and the Father are one, and because of this
> oneness I have a hidden grace. I live by the grace of
> this hidden manna, by the grace of the inner
> indwelling Presence.

> In the assurance that I am one with the Father and all
> that the Father has is mine, I am at peace. There is
> no need for worry, fear, doubt, or anxiety, for all that
> the Father has is mine by virtue of this oneness.

Such an awareness removes all responsibility from our shoulders, and it is as if a weight falls away. Furthermore, it enables us to take the responsibility away from our parents, our relatives, or our children and place it where it really belongs: on the spirit of God that indwells us, the spirit of God that is our bread, meat, wine, and water, that is our hidden manna.

Seeing Through the Visible to the Invisible

Living in the consciousness of oneness, what a different concept of man we now entertain! As a concrete example of this, let us suppose that you are looking at me sitting on a platform, and you might think, "He up there is not just what he seems to be. There is more to him than I am seeing with my eyes." And that is correct because merely looking at my body, you would be seeing only a form, a body.

Now look a little deeper; look right up through my eyes. Behind these eyes, there sits the son of God, the presence of God, the Christ incarnate, which is my hidden manna, my secret of life. I have within me a meat, a substance, a reality that the world knows nothing of because the world cannot see It with its eyes and cannot hear It with its ears. It cannot smell It, taste It, or touch It, but looking up to the platform in that consciousness of oneness, you know that I possess It, that I have It, that this hidden manna has expressed Itself in the twenty odd books and booklets of mine that you have read, and in the hundreds of tape recordings which you have heard or may hear. You realize that all that has come through me is the outpouring of an inner Spirit.

Now at the same time remember that with the physical eyes you are seeing that I am flesh and blood as you are, born with all the limitations with which you were born, and with more than some of you. Then you will know that what you are beholding in me on the platform through spiritual discernment is an image of yourself because God is no respecter of persons. All that the Father has given to me, He has given to you. Humanly, I have never deserved it any more than you have. It came to me as a gift of God in the beginning through recognition. It was given to you, also, in the beginning and it is locked up within you, too, awaiting release.

Open out a way for the "imprisoned splendor" to escape. Do not expect it to come to you from outside. Open out a way by opening the door and admitting the spirit of God which is already dwelling within you. Let the spirit of God bear witness with your spirit that you and the Father are one. Now see what kind of a concept of man you have, how the form disappears or becomes only a shell.

Enlarging Your Concept of Yourself

Automobile manufacturers know that too many persons buy automobiles because of their bright, shiny appearance.

They are fooled by that, often walking out of the showroom without too much concern as to what the mechanism of the automobile really is. We, too, are fooled by appearances, by outer bodies which are merely shells, instead of discerning the inside "machinery," the inside Spirit which I am. As you bear witness to this, your respect for me increases because you are no longer respecting a person but are beginning to discern the spirit of God that animates the person.

Now take the next step and understand that when you discern the *I* or Spirit within any person, you are witnessing a reflection of your own Self because that same *I* is also the truth about you. When you look in the mirror, you do not see you: you see the shell, the body, the casing, and regardless of how you polish it, it never becomes anything more than the shell. The important part is you, and this *you* is a selfhood that is one with the divine selfhood individually expressed. God constitutes your selfhood. The spirit of God is the animating influence of your life, soul, mind, and being. This gives you a tremendously enhanced concept of yourself.

Entering into the Presence of the Living God

Begin to know your Self. Lift up your concept of what constitutes man and you will discover God: God as my Self, God as your Self, God as the Self of friend and enemy. In doing this, the question must arise, "Ah, but I would like to know a little more about that God as well as about my Self. What is this God with whom I am one?" Then is when you enter the age of reason, real reason, spiritual reason because now you are compelled to release every concept of God that you have ever entertained. You are compelled now to forget the God who seemingly withholds good and sometimes gives good—not too often, once in a while, but mostly withholds good. You will release the concept of a God that rewards or punishes, and be assured that just as there is no God that punishes, there is no

God that rewards. Just as there is no God that withholds, there is no God that gives.

God is the same yesterday, today, and forever, the same from everlasting to everlasting, the same to the saint as to the sinner. There is no distinction of time, place, or person in God's love or God's grace. God is even the same after the experience of death as before, for "neither death, nor life. . . shall be able to separate us from the love of God,"[8] the life of God the spirit of God, or the presence of God.

As you attain a higher concept of God and of man and as your friends and relatives leave you by what is called death, but which is merely a passing into the invisible, you will bid them God-speed, knowing that they are no more out of God's sight, out of God's love, or out of God's grace than when they were visibly with you. In fact, they may be more aware of it after passing than before. Often the very act of shedding this material concept of body releases a person from the limitations of physical sense and enables him to perceive more accurately the things of God, the nature of God, and the presence of God.

Every concept of God that you have ever entertained must go. If you have believed that God is love, this must go; if you have believed that God is spirit, this must go; until one by one you shed every concept of God you have ever entertained and finally come to the place where you have no concepts whatsoever of God. When you reach that place where you are shorn of every concept of God, you are in the presence of the living God. Until then you are separated by that word in your mind which stands for God, whatever that word may be, because that word represents only a concept of God, and that concept of God will separate you from the experience of God.

Illumination as a Freedom from All Concepts

"They have taken away the Lord"[9] was spoken in a moment of illumination. All concepts of God had disappeared, and the individual was standing stark naked of concepts, free of limited and limiting concepts to realize God's presence Itself.

You might have an experience of this nature for yourself if, for a few minutes, you think of someone who is not at this moment physically present with you and, as you are thinking of him, instantly your concept of him is with you. Assume it is someone you love: wife, husband, child, mother, father, or friend. You have a pleasurable feeling because you are entertaining a pleasurable concept of the person. Now for a moment think that there may be someone who does not entertain this concept of him and who does not love him. Then you will see that you are not experiencing the reality of this person: you are experiencing your concept of him. If that same person appeared to someone else, there might not be the same effect.

You have been brought up with concepts of God, mostly erroneous ones, and the moment you think of God you think in terms of your concepts. For this reason some of you have a great deal of pleasure when you think of God. It is a rewarding experience because you have been taught comforting and wonderful things about God. But there are those of you who, at some time or other, have dreaded the very thought of the word God because God may have been presented to you as a God of vengeance, a God of punishment, or as a God of the many concepts that are presented in different religious teachings. So God brings forth a very unpleasant response in some persons.

Now remove all those concepts and agree that you, yourself, do not really know God. You know only what you have read, what you have been taught, or what you have thought about God. But that is not knowing God. You have never come face to face with God, nor have you ever experienced God when God is clothed with your concepts. Therefore, you must discard every concept of God you have entertained until there is not a single word left in your thought with which to describe God, not a single synonym left, until even the word God itself disappears and nothing at all is left in the mind. In that moment you will be face to face with the experience of God. In that moment you and the Father will have become consciously one. Then you will know above all things why you cannot know yourself. You can only *be* yourself. You can only *live* yourself.

You cannot know yourself as if it were someone external to you. You cannot objectify yourself and say, "Oh, I know me out here," because the "me" out here is not "me." The "me" is *I* inside, looking out here. So you will understand that you cannot know God with your mind because you cannot know God out here. You cannot have a picture of God; you cannot have a thought of God. You cannot have even an image, a vision, or an idea of God because the Knower is God, not the known—the Knower. But the Knower and the known are one.

The Mystery of God as Individual Consciousness

When you realize that "That which I am seeking I am,"[10] then you will know how Moses could understand in a flash that it was the "I Am That I Am"[11] that he was seeking. You will know why Jesus taught, "I am the bread of life.[12]. . . I have meat to eat that ye know not of.[13]. . . I am the resurrection and the life."[14] You will know why I cannot *know* eternal life because *I am* eternal. You will know why I cannot have bread. You will know why I cannot receive from God because *I* am the embodiment of all that God has and is. *I* am life eternal. This is the mystery of the revelation of God as individual consciousness.

> I cannot know life eternal; I cannot get life eternal;
> I cannot get health; I cannot get supply;
> I cannot get companionship: I am these,
> I am, I embody, I embrace these within
> my own being, and that is the reason I cannot
> demonstrate, get, or attain them.
> I have meat that ye know not of. I am life eternal.

I cannot be resurrected: I am the resurrection.
I cannot attain immortality: I am immortal. I am
immortal being because I and the Father are one.
God's being and my being are one being. All that the
Father has is mine. "Son, thou are ever with me, and
all that I have is thine." [15]

Do you see that spiritual discernment lies in knowing the infinite nature of man because of his relationship with infinity? Spiritual discernment reveals the eternal nature of man because it reveals the eternality of divine Being and his oneness with that divine Being.

Spiritual life is a revelation. It is a revelation within yourself of the nature of your being. Spiritual life is not attaining something outside or gaining something. It is not a means of achieving something. The spiritual life is a continuous revelation within, a revelation of the nature of your being, a revelation of the nature of your identity.

When you know yourself, you will know God, for there is no God separate and apart from you. Therefore, until you realize that the nature of a spiritual message is really a revelation or unfoldment from within, you will miss the way because you will be seeking some attainment in the without. You do not attain in the without. Whatever comes to you in the without is the added thing that comes of seeking and finding the kingdom of God within yourself.

The Rebirth

Begin your meditation by remembering that the spirit of God is already within you, knocking at the door of your consciousness. By an act of commitment and an invitation, open the door of your consciousness to admit this Spirit. With the continuous practice of a meditation of this kind, there comes a specific moment in your life when the new birth takes place, when the spirit of God announces Itself within you, sometimes reminding you, "I will never leave thee, nor forsake thee,"[16] or "I will be with thee until the end of the world," or "Take no further thought for your life for *I* am here."

In one way or another there comes a specific moment when that which is dormant in you is revived, when the rebirth or the resurrection takes place. Actually the spirit of God is never dormant. It is you and I who are dormant and who in some moment of awareness awaken to the glory that is already present. There is no such thing as a dormant spirit of God or a dormant Christ. There are dormant senses which must be awakened. "Awake thou that sleepest,"[17] not "Awake the Christ," but "Awake thou, the mortal senses, thou that sleepest, and Christ that is omnipresence will be thy light."

As long as you are trying to know yourself out here in the body, you will fail. As long as you are trying to know God up here in the mind, you will fail, for God is not objective to you. God is the Self of you. The seeker and the sought are one. This is the meaning of the stories of the search for the Holy Grail. The searchers for the Holy Grail went out looking all over the world for it. It was never discovered there. Always it was discovered upon the return home, and home means consciousness. It is discovered the moment you return to your own consciousness and realize, "That which I have been seeking, I am; that which I have looked for in books, mountains, and temples, I am. I was really seeking my Self. I was searching for my Self, and when I found my Self, I found God."

This is really the sum and substance of the spiritual life. The spiritual life has nothing to do with looking for spiritual powers, seeking miracles, or changing the outer aspects of your life. True, that was the decoy that brought you to this search. Something missing in your outer life set up a vacuum, and you began to search for what would fill the vacuum. That is the decoy that ultimately reveals to you that you are not going to find it until you find *Me* in you, the *I* within. Then as you abide in *Me* and let *Me* abide in you, as you realize *I* as the very center of your being, the very soul of your being, the spirit of God in you, all thought about this outer world disappears, and automatically the world begins to change as an externalization of that state of consciousness which has now been attained.

The World Reflects Back to You What You Give Out

Your outer experience is the direct manifestation of your inner state of consciousness. Therefore, the outer world can be no better to you than the degree of your present state of consciousness. If you are not satisfied with your outer world, it means that you must seek further for more light as to your identity and for more light as to the nature of God. As you attain these, the outer world changes accordingly.

The outer world reflects back to you your state of consciousness, and you can begin to prove this within twenty-four or forty-eight hours. I asked you to look up at me on this platform and not look at this framework, this body, or casing, but try to look through my eyes and find *Me,* try to discern that which is behind my eyes. See if you cannot find something about me that is invisible, intangible, and different from what you have ever thought of before.

Then begin to make a practice of this. But it must be done silently, secretly, and sacredly. It must never be done openly. Begin to look at the members of your family—husband, wife, child, parent, aunt, uncle, cousins—one by one. Never try to do this for them as a group. Just take one person at a time and forget all that you know about him. Forget his appearance and see if you can discern something within him that is not evident to your five physical senses. See if you cannot discern something in him that God planted there in the beginning before ever the world was. After that gradually spread this silent influence and take in the neighbors and the friends, and the storekeepers, the office-workers, and everyone with whom you come in contact.

You will have a wonderful opportunity as all the candidates for office in the next election come before your gaze. Do not pay too much attention to what they are saying because they are not going to tell you the truth. That would not be good politics. Try to look through the appearance and see what you can discern of the nature of God in them, the nature of their manhood, the stature of their manhood.

The miracle that you will discover is the different way in which the world is treating you. It will really be a miracle-experience when you find that the world no longer treats you as it has in the past. It cannot. The world can reflect back to you only that which you are giving out. As you begin to perceive the nature of the stature of manhood in Christ Jesus, that is, the spiritual nature of my being, his being, and her being, you compel them to bear witness to the spirit of God in you.

ACROSS THE DESK

"Arise, shine; for thy light is come, and the glory of the Lord is risen upon thee." This is the miracle of Easter. The resurrection of Jesus symbolizes the possibility of the Christ, the "light," the "glory of the Lord" being raised up in each and every one. When that happens in you, you have experienced Easter.

Today there is much talk about miracles being performed by individuals. In fact, we seem to be living in an age of miracle-talk. But let us not be hypnotized by the appearance. Joel clearly and emphatically points out the necessity of seeing through the good appearance as well as the bad. What are most so-called miracles but a good appearance? Is this what we as Infinite Way students look for? No, we reject the appearance and perceive that the real miracle, unseen to the human eye, is Thy light, Thy grace, the glory of God rising within, dissolving human consciousness.

As the realized Christ-consciousness breaks through, real

miracles appear and we see the miracle of God's grace. Then we rejoice in the miracle of Easter every day.

TAPE RECORDED EXCERPTS
Prepared by the Editor

It requires a real right-about-face to be able to turn away from the universally accepted belief that life has a beginning and that with each passing day we are drawing closer to its ending. This is partly because we believe that we are body instead of understanding that we have a body and that the life we are, formed the body as an instrument. The recognition and realization of life as eternal, from everlasting to everlasting, without beginning or end, and never dependent upon form, comes as we gain an understanding of the Source of life and of our inseparability from that Source.

The following excerpts from the tape recordings will help in attaining and living out from that consciousness of immortality here and now.

"Life"

"When you have caught a tiny glimpse of. . . your life not being entombed in your body, you will understand the story of the Resurrection. They had Jesus entombed and confined in a tomb, all sealed up just like our bodies. . . . But when they looked he was not there. He had risen.

"Human beings are entombed. . . . The Resurrection is the story of the Christ, your divine Self, entombed in a body. . . and the Resurrection is when the realization comes to you:

I never was there. 'I and my Father are one.'
I live and move and have my being in God, not in a
material concept, not in a womb. I live and move and
have my being in God, in Spirit. I dwell in the secret

place of the most High. I abide in the word of God,
and the word of God abides in me, not in the body.

There is no place in the body where you could hide the word of God, but the word of God does abide in you. . . .

"When you begin to perceive that truth spiritually, you will be able to look at this body and say, 'Now I perceive that *I,* that very *I* that I have been meditating upon, was given dominion over this body. *I* was given dominion over everything on earth, beneath the earth, and above the earth. *I* have dominion over this body, *I* govern it; *I* feed it; *I* care for it. It is my possession.'

"By realizing that, you take your body out of this world where it has been at the mercy of weather, climate, food, and calendars that testify to the passing of time. You take your body out of the carnal mind by realizing that this body is your precious possession, given you of the Father. But you were given dominion. You were given charge of it, not to turn it over to calendars or to the control of wind and weather. You were given it to care for. . . .

"Your body is responding to influences outside of you over which you have no control unless you have begun to perceive the nature of *I,* and then get hold of this body: 'No more wandering out here in a human world. You live in me, and *I* govern you. *I* am not in the body: the body is in me. . . and subject to my government and control.' . . . There could be no truth at all to immortality if this body were you. There must be Something besides this body."

Joel S. Goldsmith, "The Secret of the Resurrection," *The 1958 London Open Class.*

"You are something separate and apart from your body, just as much separate and apart from your body as you are separate and apart from your automobile. . . . This *I* which I am and which you are is permanently here, eternally here. . . . Perceiving that, you will know why God is your true identity because only

God is immortal; only God is eternal. The nature of God, Consciousness, is a continued state of immortality, of eternal being, of eternality, and that is what I am. . . . a state of divine consciousness.

"This that I am and you are, which is immortal, is likewise infinite, and so you will realize, through this, that you are never using up your life. You are never using up your strength; you are never using up your span of years. The only you there is exists as consciousness. . . .

"Since death is the last enemy to be overcome, if you will perceive this point of your true identity as the consciousness which permeates this body, which uses this body as an instrument or vehicle, you will come into the experience that you witness in nature: you will shed this body, not by death but by the shedding of the skin or the shedding of the nails, the shedding of the hair, or the shedding of the atoms or parts that make up the organs and functions of the body with a constant renewal."

Joel S. Goldsmith, "The Invisible Nature of Your Life," *The 1955 First Kailua Study Group.*

Chapter Five

Nothing Takes Place
Outside of Consciousness

One of the most important principles of the Infinite Way is that God constitutes individual being. This means that God constitutes your being and mine. God manifests as our life, mind, spirit, and soul. Even our body is the temple of God. This is the spiritual truth about every one of us.

God has given us dominion over "the fish of the sea, and over the fowl of the air, and over the cattle, and over all the earth, and over every creeping thing that creepeth upon the earth."[1] God created us in His own image, giving us His life, soul, spirit, and intelligence and, in so doing, He gave us dominion over ignorance, superstition, and darkness. This dominion is our spiritual birthright and makes us a law unto our life's demonstration.

All Error, a Mental Imposition

We are human beings because we have forfeited our birthright of dominion and turned it over to what the Master called "this world."[2] At the very instant that the newspapers, radio, or television announces an impending epidemic, human beings open themselves to becoming victims of the epidemic.

They permit it to become a part of their experience by means of mentally imposed suggestions from outside. It is not that anyone has maliciously started the rumor just to make them ill: it is in universal human consciousness, and it is thrust at all of us. Without knowing the underlying truth of being, we may passively accept it with a "Well, what can I do about it? I'm just a statistic. So if forty out of a hundred get it, I may be one of the forty." If we escape it, we consider ourselves lucky. Actually, we are responsible for being victimized by the mass hypnosis only because we do not know how to avoid it. We do not know what caused it or how to prevent it.

The Presidential election of 1916 illustrates the effect of any kind of mass hysteria. The incumbent president was re-elected because he had kept the nation out of war, clear-cut evidence that the public did not want to become involved in any European conflict. But six months later we were at war. Why? Why did a majority of the voters of the United States change their minds in six months, and beg and plead to go to war? Did the people really want war? Not any more than before.

The shift in public opinion was the result of a consistent and carefully planned program of propaganda, causing the public to reverse itself and clamor for war as a result of the mass hysteria that had been deliberately induced, a mental imposition against which an alert and informed citizenry could have defended itself.

There are impersonal mental forces operating in human consciousness, and they come to us in the guise of a person or a condition. They are thrust upon us as sinful or false appetites, as lack and limitation, or as threats of danger, and we respond. All evil reaches us through a mental imposition, and in no other way. It is never personal. Let us not blame the members of any race or religion because that would not be true. All evil is impersonal, even though it may seem to come through a person. The point is that the person who may appear to be the cause of evil in our experience is no more responsible than are we who accept an evil person or condition into our consciousness.

All error, regardless of its name or nature, all the world's discords and inharmonies, whether in the form of a sinful desire, false appetite, disease, or unemployment, come to us as a form of mental malpractice. It is an imposed mental force from outside. It is not of your doing or mine, except for the basic fault that we have surrendered our dominion. That is the original sin, and having done that, the only other reason for our discord is not that we are evil, but that we continually accept evil from the world.

Divine Sonship Makes Us a Law unto Ourselves

When we understand that God constitutes our being, that God is the very life, mind, and soul of us, then we can understand the meaning of the passage in Genesis which states that God gave man dominion over everything, even over the stars, the planets, the weather, over all that is in the air, in the sea, and beneath the sea. That dominion is ours by virtue of the fact that we were given the mind and life of God:

I am the son of God, the manifestation of God's own
being. God is revealing Itself on earth as my being,
manifesting as my mind, my life, my soul, and my
spirit, and even as the law unto my being.

No law can operate upon me.
All law must operate out from and through me.
Only the law of God can operate in, on,
and through my consciousness, and nothing from
without can enter that defiles or makes a lie.

Once we see ourselves as children of God and under the law of God, nothing and no one, either individually or collectively, can influence us. We will not then respond to urges from without. We will be a law unto ourselves, a law of God, not a law of selfishness using our mind to benefit ourselves at somebody else's expense, but a law of love, a law of intelligence, and a law of life.

This, we cannot do unless we can perceive that God made us in His image and likeness, that God made us of the very substance and fiber of His own being, and we thereby and therefore are under the law of God.

> The law of God manifests in my soul and
> spirit. The law of God moves in my inward parts.
> The law of God manifests in my mind and body.
> The law of God establishes me, maintains and sus-
> tains me free from external influences.

When we establish ourselves in that way, we are the law unto our life. All things begin to "work together for good to them that love God,"[3] to those that love this idea of being God-governed and not subject to outside influences.

Every student must study well, read, ponder, and meditate within himself until he comes to an absolute conviction that God made all that was made, and all that God made is good. If he believes that there is any evil, he is accepting a suggestion external to his own being, a suggestion from outside, from the carnal mind which is the universal belief in two powers. When he accepts the suggestion of a selfhood apart from God, a law or a life apart from God, he is accepting a mental imposition from without.

The Impersonal Nature of Malpractice

If we understand this, we can understand why and what mental malpractice is. It is only if we think of mental malpractice as the act of a person or group of persons that we find ourselves in trouble. To identify malpractice with a person is to personalize evil, and we will suffer for believing that it is a person.

It is not possible to suffer from the thoughts of others, if we have accepted ourselves as one with God. Only if we surrender our dominion can we suffer from the thoughts of others.

The thoughts of others do not have power except where there is a belief that they are power as is illustrated in the religions of primitive races. Insofar as our knowledge is concerned, their religion never rose above the mental level, and therefore, consisted of both good and evil. There were the priests who prayed for health and brought forth health; they prayed for harmony and brought forth harmony. They were a blessing and a benediction to their people. But in every one of these tribes there was also the evil priest, and this one, in the minds of his tribe, was endowed with the power of cursing and of killing. As we study these ancient teachings, we find that the good priests really could heal, and the evil priests could kill.

Until a hundred years ago, such practices were carried on in the Hawaiian Islands, where there were good kahunas and bad kahunas. From childhood the people were taught that the good kahuna could heal and the bad kahuna could kill, and therefore all their lives they lived in fear of the bad kahunas. This was true in Central and South America in the days of the primitive peoples there. It was true in Egypt, in Australia among the aborigines, and today among the voodoos of Haiti.

Becoming Free of Personal Malpractice

Even today, if a person can find those who are susceptible to the belief that somebody's thought can hurt him, so it is. Perhaps that is why metaphysicians are among the easiest persons to malpractice: they believe in it, some of them at least. But those who do not accept that superstition cannot be touched. They are not affected in any way whatsoever.

There is not a divine mind and a mortal mind. There are not two minds. There is only one mind, the instrument of God, and its power is good. There is no power in what is called malpractice, albeit there is power in the *belief* that it has power. That is the only power it has.

Nobody's thought can hurt us individually or collectively, because the malpractitioner's thought is merely the effect of the belief in two powers. It is not the one mind; it cannot be the one mind because it is based on the belief in two powers, good and evil. To understand this would save us from any form of what is called personal or directed malpractice.

Becoming Free of Universal Malpractice

Furthermore, we must go beyond freeing ourselves from personal malpractice to freeing ourselves from that universal malpractice which appears as a belief in infection, contagion, or heredity. We do this by understanding that the universal belief in the power of disease cannot operate in, on, or through our consciousness because *God is our consciousness,* and nothing can operate on God. Nothing can enter God-consciousness that "defileth. . . or maketh a lie."[4] Therefore if God constitutes our consciousness, we are immune to the malpractice resulting from the belief in good and evil.

To the pure, all things are pure. If there is nothing in our consciousness to respond to evil, no evil can take root there. But how do we make ourselves free of evil? In one way, and one way alone: by living and moving and having our being in the realization of God as constituting our consciousness, our mind, soul, and our being, as our very life. Nothing of a discordant nature, then, can enter that mind, that soul, or that life. All superstitions, rumors, or reports about weather, climate, health, infection, contagion, or epidemics are nothing but imposed mental suggestions, and we are not subject to them because they are not power.

The Infinite Way states that sin, disease, and death are not power. They are only imposed suggestions stemming from the belief in two powers: the Adamic belief in good and evil. The evils and discords of this world do not come forth from Consciousness, for Consciousness is the source of intelligence. To know that their only basis is in universal belief, the carnal mind, makes their nothingness clear.

Let us be very sure, however, that we are not believing that carnal mind is really mind. Carnal mind, or mortal mind, means a belief in two powers, a universal belief, not a personal one: not your belief, not my belief, not his belief, not her belief, but an impersonal universal belief. When we know this, then we can laugh at it as heartily as we would if someone told us, "Oh, there's a man down there who is going to think you to death." No one could do that because we understand that God is our life, and nobody can think God away, so therefore we stand firm in that realization.

God is the health of our countenance. What can enter that countenance to destroy or impair its perfection? But we must *know* this truth. We must know the truth of our true identity. Then we must know the source of error, which is not our wrong thinking, nor any of the beliefs we have picked up. The source of all error is a universal malpractice, a universal suggestion or imposition coming to us for acceptance, just as the devil came to Jesus to tempt him. To this devil, Jesus said, "Get thee behind me, Satan."[5] And to our devil, appearing in the form of infection or contagion, poverty or unhappiness, we have to say, "I recognize you as suggestion."

A small group of students has experimented with the phenomenon of weather appearing in the form of tidal waves and typhoons, and, through knowing that every unnatural condition of weather is nothing but mental malpractice, has watched them dissolve and disappear in space. It is not at the North or the South Pole that a condition of weather starts. It starts in a universal belief in two powers, and it is stopped when it hits up against the realization of one power. That one power is the spirit of God in us, the presence of God, and the life of God in us.

Nothing can enter our experience except through our consciousness. If there is a rumor of a storm, it has to wedge itself into our consciousness before it can become manifest. Two or more gathered together in the truth, "ten"[6] righteous men, can save a city.

Error, an Imposed Suggestion

It takes but very little realization of truth to wipe out the evils of this world as they touch our individual consciousness. Let us always remember that we cannot experience anything that does not enter our consciousness. But anything can enter our consciousness unless we are alert and watchful.

Those round about us see our body, but there is another part of us that no one sees: our mind. Our mind is invisible; and behind the invisibility of our mind, we stand. There is an I of each one of us; there is a mind, and there is a body. I have a mind. I have a body, and I am standing back here and addressing my mind, and it in turn governs my body. My body cannot catch cold. Any cold that enters my body must first enter through my mind, and that means I have let it in. That is but one evidence of how important I am in my life. I stand behind me. I stand behind my mind, and behind my body.

> Since I and the Father are one, the qualities
> and the quantities of the Father are mine.
> I am the fulfillment of all that God is, and
> nothing from without can enter my consciousness
> that "defileth. . . or maketh a lie" because I stand here
> in the realization of God as my being.

Impersonal Nature of Evil

By consciously identifying ourselves with God, we open ourselves to all that God is. By recognizing error as an imposed suggestion from without we "nothingize" it.

We do not need God to get rid of error for us. It is only necessary to know the universal nature of that which is claiming to impose itself upon us from without, and its nothingness. When we are asked for help and do not fasten the error on to our patient, but impersonalize it, the patient will have a healing. All that holds any person bound to a disease is the personalization of evil.

Evil begins with the Adamic belief in two powers, coming to us as a suggestion, a suggestion of one thing or another, which we admit into our consciousness. Afterwards, we try to get rid of it. How much better would it be to keep the lock on the door and keep the thief of suggestion out, rather than setting out to get rid of him after he is in.

Not Affirmations and Denials but Realization

Two principles of the Infinite Way, which can change our entire life, are to know our real identity and to understand all evil as a mental imposition. Let us begin to know our own identity and not fear to claim our sonship with God, for in our true identity we are divine being. The essence of us is God. The very life and fiber of our being is God. All that constitutes our being is God. This, we can demonstrate in proportion as we realize that all the negative things of life—sin, disease, death, lack, and limitation—are imposed beliefs. They are superimposed upon us, and we accept them through ignorance; whereas the truth is that because God is too pure to behold iniquity, nothing is true that comes to our consciousness unless it testifies to immortality, eternality, infinity, and abundance.

We know the truth, and in our knowing of the truth we are also knowing the nothingness of the error. But we do not use affirmations and denials in the form of "I am rich and I know it! I am rich and I know it!" and then have to open up our purse and say, "I can't find a dollar in it!" In the same way, there is no use in saying, "I am well! I am well! I am well," if we are sick.

Not at all. That is only a form of hypnotism. It was used by Coué in the days of Couéism. "Every day and in every way I am getting better and better." Some metaphysicians went even further when they looked into their empty pocketbook or at their sick body and declared, "I am rich. I am perfect!"

In the Infinite Way we do not recite a prayer a hundred times, and then expect that the hundredth time we repeat it the evil will be gone. We do not repeat and repeat it for the purpose of making something happen. But we do consciously remember the truth of our being.

Let us think of the meaning of that word *I*. We may remember that Jesus said, "I am the bread of life.[7]. . . I am the light of the world.[8]. . . I am the way, the truth, and the life.[9]. . . I am the resurrection, and the life."[10] How wonderful that *I* is!

> I in the midst of me is mighty.
> I is the way, the truth, and the life.
> All this error that appears as limitation, finiteness,
> negativeness, this is carnal mind,
> nothingness, the "arm of flesh."[11]
> This is a universal belief in two powers.
> But I is the only power. And that I in the midst of
> me embodies all the God-power there is.
> I cannot use It: It can use me.
> If I am still, I in the midst of me will live my life.

Although there have been many mystics in the history of the world, very few of them were healers. As a matter of fact, some of the mystics suffered greatly, physically and mentally, and this may be because they never understood the source of evil, its nature, or how it operates. The truth is that evil operates as a mesmeric suggestion which in our ignorance we accept. It operates as a universal malpractice, as an imposed belief in two powers. But it cannot operate when we know that God constitutes our being, that all that God is, we are, and that nothing except the qualities and quantities of God can enter our consciousness.

The Impersonal Nature of Good

In proportion as we realize the impersonal nature of evil, we will also recognize the impersonal nature of good. We will never be guilty of saying, "I am good"; "I am spiritual"; "I am charitable"; "I am forgiving"; or "I am loving." Things like that will never again enter our mind. Whatever qualities of good are manifest through us are qualities of God finding expression and outlet through us or through anyone else. As long as we are claiming virtue for ourselves, we are perpetuating the Adam-dream. The Master said, "Why callest thou me good? there is none good but one, that is, God.[12]. . . I can of mine own self do nothing.[13]. . . The Father that dwelleth in me, he doeth the works." [14]

As we arrive at a state of consciousness in which we know that we are but the showing forth of God, the instrument through which, or as which, God appears on earth, and that every good quality is not ours, but God manifesting through us, then we shall begin to see how these grow in quantity and quality.

To impersonalize good means to understand that we have no health of our own. God is the health of our countenance. It means to know that we have no wealth. "The earth is the Lord's, and the fulness thereof,"[15] but it is comforting to know "Son. . . all that I have is thine."[16] At least we have the use of it, even though we know that at the end of the line, there is a probate court where we check all our belongings. Our material possessions are ours only for a day. Nevertheless they are ours in abundance if we realize that they come, not from the grace of me or the grace of you, but from the grace of God. That is impersonalizing good.

When we can do that, we can also impersonalize evil. Then if we do see an intoxicated person, a thief, a slanderer, or a scandalmonger, we will not pin the evil on to him. We will realize that this, too, is nothing but personalization, in this case a per-sonalization of error. It is the belief that a person of himself can be good or evil. The truth is that all evil is an imposition from a universal malpractice, whereas all good is an emanation of God.

Across the Desk

Integrity is the backbone of all relationships. And these days what a crying need there is for integrity and ethical conduct at all levels of human experience! Integrity is a spiritual quality and stems from God just as do love and gratitude.

As we maintain our oneness with God by turning within continually during the day, the integrity of our actions is assured, and with integrity as the basis, our everyday relation-ships are strengthened and harmonized. We experience the beauty and joy of oneness with each other as a result of our real-ized oneness with God. As with understanding and peace in a family or community, so integrity among nations, in govern-ment, business, and family relationships always begins with the individual. How much integrity are you showing forth?

Tape Recorded Excerpts
Prepared by the Editor

This tape recorded excerpt is a continuation of the material on "Life" which began in the April letter.

"Life"

"As we attain the realization of our true identity as an invis-ible life, when we look in the mirror we no longer say, 'Look what I look like,' we say, 'Oh, my body needs a little adjusting up somewhere.' We do not identify what we see in the mirror with ourselves because that is not *I*. That is our body. The very moment that I realize *I,* my body begins to change form. The body only looks like what it does. . . because we, ignorantly, have been identifying that body as ourselves. Through false identification, we have made this body look like what it looks like; whereas, with right identification, we can quickly begin to change its nature so that we can say ten years from now that we look ten years younger than we look now. It can be so, and in many cases it is so, and in every case of realization it is to some degree so. . . . Out of the consciousness of God cannot come age, limitation, weakness, or death.

"This house [body] must be renewed day by day, season by season, by the realization that I am not what appears outwardly. I am the spiritual life force which is functioning from the within to the without. It is not that I have a life-force: *I* am that life-force. That life force constitutes my true and individual being. The more I realize that, the more it flows in harmonious and infinite forms and varieties."

Joel S. Goldsmith, "The Invisible Nature of Your Life,"
The 1955 First Kailua Study Group.

"There is no difference between the flow of God this minute or a hundred years from now. It is just a matter of the continuity of the contact. Actually the life of God will never end, and as long as there is a work for us to do on what is called this plane of existence, we can maintain ourselves here on this plane by the contact. And I do not mean as doddering old people either: I mean in the vitality of strength, youth, health, and wholeness. But we can do it by that contact because It, Itself, is the presence and power that does it. We cannot remain here one minute longer after the call has come to labor in other vineyards.

"The degree of experienced life is in proportion to the degree of consciousness unfolding. Regardless of where you are this moment in life, the degree of it represents your degree of

God-life expressed or unfolded in conscious expression, and you can change it by opening out your consciousness for a greater flow."

Joel S. Goldsmith, "The Deep Pool of Our Being," *The 1955 Kailua Study Group.*

"We are unfolding states of one infinite consciousness, and therefore, we are appearing to human sense in, let us say, this stage of spiritual development now. Now then, there is nothing that was born that must not die. There is nothing that had a beginning that must not have an ending. The shell of us disappears, just as every year our bodies change. The skin sloughs off, the blood cells change, and there is a continuous dying and rebirthing of all of our bodies. Every year this process goes on.

"Outwardly this is not death although it is just the same as death. Every part of our body dies; every part of our body is reborn; and one of these days this shell probably drops away from us, and immediately begins to make its reappearance with another shell. That is all happening in the second chapter of Genesis where there are these mechanical processes of conception and birth. They are not happening in reality. . . .

"Close your eyes and gently say, 'I.' Now go back in your history five years and see if you can place yourself where you were five years ago, and say, 'I.' See if that is not the same I that you voiced. Now go back twenty years, and see if you can visualize yourself as you looked twenty years ago and in what part of the country you were at that time. Look out at some of the scenery that was close to you twenty years ago. . . . Isn't it the same I that looked out through your eyes?. . .

"The only thing that is changed is your outer form and the knowledge that you have acquired over these years. But were not you the same person? Isn't that the same I? You didn't change 'I' anywhere on that journey. . . . If you could go back you would find that at your birth you were the same I that you are now, if

you could have said, 'I' at that time. . . . Your body has grown. . .
but it is the same identical I.

"Now, let us come back to this present minute and look
out and say, 'I.' See if you cannot identify with the same 'I'
back there. If we look ahead ten years, do you not see that it
is the same I that is going to look out of there. . . . Ten years
from now some of us will have passed on, but that same I is
going to be right there looking on. You can do anything you
want with this body, but you cannot do anything to *I*. Twenty
years from now, fifty years from now, that *I* is going to be just
as intact as it is now and just as young and just as vital as it is
now. It is not going to age or change. It is going to be the same
I. That is your identity."

Joel S. Goldsmith, "Spiritual Unfoldment, Not Human Birth,"
The Second 1958 Chicago Closed Class.

"We never discard our form, our concept of form. . . . Yet *I*
go on forever, and *I* always have form, *I* am always embodied as
form. *I* can never lose my form any more than *I* can lose my
identity.

"As human beings, we are the tomb in which the Christ is
buried. All that the world sees is this corpse that we are walking around in. Within us, in this tomb of human selfhood, is
the Christ, and in certain moments of our lives, . . . an experience takes place, and then when we look in the mirror we
will recognize:

> I am not here any more. I am risen. I am no longer
> buried in the tomb of a body. I am no longer subject
> to its limitations. . . . I am no longer in the tomb of
> finite belief. I am no longer entombed in the body of
> matter. . . . These are my servants; these are the tools
> given me for my everyday life, for I know myself
> now: I am he. I am the child of God, heir of God. . . .

I have been given dominion over this body and over
every body under the sea, on the land, and in the air.
I am free. I have found my freedom in my
Christhood. In the realization of my true identity as
I, I am free. . . and I no longer
live under the law, but under Grace."

Joel S. Goldsmith, "The Mystical I,"
The Second Chicago 1958 Closed Class.

"Dying does not ensure immortality. Immortality is an
activity of truth in your consciousness and can just as well be
experienced while you are on earth as in any future lifetime. In
order to experience immortality, you must understand the
nature of your own being. Unless you know what you are, you
cannot experience immortality. . . .

"The longer you permit the world belief to handle you, that
this body is you, the longer it will control you and the longer it
will make you believe that with the change of body you die. You
did not die when you left infancy; you did not die when you left
childhood; you did not die when you came to maturity. You
merely witnessed these changes of your body, and you are going
to go on witnessing changes of body unto eternity. But always
you will remain in your full and complete identity. You will
always be individual you. You will always have the integrity of
the fullness of your being, and you will arise into the fullness of
the stature of manhood in Christ Jesus when you acknowledge:

'I and my Father are one.'
Therefore I am indestructible—indestructible, indivisible, inseparable from Life, from Love, from Being.

"Until you realize this, you cannot fully benefit from the
teaching of the Master because the teaching of the Master is that
the life of God is your life, and this constitutes your immortal-

ity. . . . Immortality is an experience which you may have here and now in this very moment if you can say to yourself, within yourself: 'I. "I and my Father are one," and the I that I am is of the same spiritual substance as God. The *I* that I am is of the same truth-substance of God. The *I* that I am is of the same love substance of God. Therefore the *I* that I am is incorporeal, spiritual, pure, infinite, and It has manifested, It has given me this body to live it.'

"Do not wait for immortality to come at some later time. If you are not experiencing it in this room now, . . . retire into a meditation in which you realize the omnipresence of the life of God as your life, and thereby experience immortality. If you do not succeed tonight, go peacefully and quietly to sleep, but remember that tomorrow you owe yourself a debt, and that is to return again to meditation, to the realization of the omnipresence of the life of God as your life. Continue this whether it takes a day, a week, a month, or a year. Continue until the 'still small voice' says to you, 'I will never leave you, nor forsake you for I am come that you might have life eternally.' Then you will be living in your immortality."

Joel S. Goldsmith, "Spiritual Discernment, Through Meditation, Reveals the Kingdom of God," *The 1963 Manchester Work.*

Chapter Six

I, If I Be Lifted Up

The Infinite Way is based on the premise that our state of consciousness draws to us our life-experience. We are responsible for whatever of good comes into our lives. Nobody can give it to us because it is not separate and apart from our consciousness. We draw it to ourselves.

Moreover, and this is not easy to swallow and digest, whatever of discord and inharmony we have experienced in life, we have created for ourselves. Nobody has done it to us, and nothing has brought it to us except ourselves. We may not be willing to accept or believe this as we think back over our life because the tendency is usually to blame someone else for our own shortcomings: "Oh, no, it was my parents' situation that prevented me from getting an education"; "It was my partner's failure that caused me to lose a fortune"; "It was my husband's lack of consideration that made me unhappy"; or "It was my wife's extravagance that increased my worry." None of this is true. Hard as this is to acknowledge, nevertheless, our state of consciousness has drawn to us the experiences that we have had or are now having.

That does not imply that there should be any guilt upon our shoulders for wrong doing or wrong thinking. It only indicates our ignorance of the truth, but the truth was not always available to us. In fact, there was very little of truth for anyone to know until modern metaphysical teachings brought a measure of light.

There is a God, and wherever the spirit of that God is, there is liberty. But it takes a *you* or a *me* to bring that spirit of God into active expression where we are. We must not look to God for our good any more than we must look to "man, whose breath is in his nostrils."[1] But we must know the truth. "Ye shall know the truth, and the truth shall make you free."[2] This puts the responsibility on your shoulders and on mine, for unless you and I know the truth, we shall not be made free and we cannot help free those to whom we owe that obligation.

Although God is the same yesterday, today, and forever and is no respecter of persons, there is a "ye": "*Ye* shall know the truth." In proportion to your state of consciousness, do you bring harmony to your body, home, family, purse, community, and ultimately to your entire world.

Coming into Obedience to God's Law

Any discord or inharmony that exists in our experience or that may come into it represents in some degree our disobedience to God's law or violation of it. It does not mean that we are always responsible because there are things which we may not yet know. Nevertheless, the penalty is going to be the same. Ignorance is no excuse.

Before we can take the final step of receiving the Holy Ghost, which can only come to us after a measure of purification, we must first of all purify ourselves by coming into obedience to certain laws of spiritual living.

In what ways are we not pure? Let us begin with a minor step. Are we agreed that no man on earth is our father and that there is only one Father? We may have to spend quite a few months with that particular passage because, if we accept literally the fatherhood of God, we have to wipe out of our consciousness racial, religious, and national barriers—and this not with lip service. There must be an actual coming into the realization that there is only one creative Principle which created this universe in Its own image and likeness, and therefore, we in our true identity are brothers and sisters, whether Greek or Jew, bond or free.

Some of those brothers and sisters at this moment are good and some are bad, but we pray for the bad ones even more than for the good ones because they need it more. And how shall we pray? Will our prayers be that they prosper in their evil ways? No, our prayers will be that the spirit of God awaken them so that they, too, may come into this brotherhood of realized souls. We pray that the errors of envy, hate, jealousy, and mad ambition be broken in them and that the Christ be realized.

In this process of self-purification, we turn to the Master's command to forgive seventy times seven those who have offended us—personally, and then perhaps nationally and racially— and see how many weeks it takes us before we come to that place of purity where we can say, "I have forgiven seventy times seven. I have forgiven so completely that never again can I be offended by anyone or anything." It takes a lot of doing, but it must be done.

Remember, however, that these are only the minor and first steps that the Master gave us. The major ones are a little more difficult. We study the four Gospels to find out whether or not we have learned the secret of forgiving seventy times seven. We discover whether or not we have learned to pray for our enemies and really bring ourselves to the consciousness of meaning it. We examine ourselves to find out whether we are holding anyone in bondage to his errors, that is, wanting to see him punished, or whether we are releasing him.

As we study the Master's teaching further, we discover how many ways we have been violating God's law and thereby keeping ourselves from God's rain when it falls. God's rain falls, but we are out there with a pitchfork instead of a pail! God's grace was flowing, but we were not ready to receive it. Whatever measure of lack we have, we can be assured that it was because we were not there to receive God's grace as it came by. God's grace is forever flowing. We cannot start its flow by petition and we cannot stop its flow by being bad. We keep it out of our personal experience by shutting our door, and the way we shut the door is by violating those principles of spiritual living that Jesus Christ has shown us.

The Christ-way is not the old Hebraic way of an eye for an eye and a tooth for a tooth, but the way of doing good for evil. Is returning good for evil to be lip service, or is it an act which must be performed? Lip service is not enough. Action is required.

Mortals Live in a Sense of Separation from God

What is human experience but a sense of separation from God? We live as mortals who cannot please God until the spirit of God dwells in us, and only when that spirit dwells in us do we become children of God. Perhaps you have not realized that. Perhaps you have taken the absolute position that we are all children of God, just as it is true that God fills all space; but, so far as you and I are concerned, this is of no value until our sonship is a revealed activity of being. Up to that time, it is merely a potentiality.

This world is not made up of people with the attained state of consciousness of a Jesus. It is not made up of children of God. This world is made up of selfish human beings, some of whom are willing to pray for their friends, some of whom are willing to pray for anybody as long as he is good according to their particular standards of goodness.

The children of God wipe out all barriers and all distinctions. They refuse to hold any man in judgment, criticism, or condemnation, knowing that God Himself sends His rain on the just and on the unjust. They know that the Master was sent here to reveal that God has more pleasure in one sinner redeemed, one black sheep found, than in all the others.

The children of God are those who dwell consciously in the very presence of God. Remember that in an absolute sense the presence of God is in every hospital, on every battlefield, and in every place where trickery and treachery are being plotted and planned. But of what good is It? None, whatsoever, except where the Presence is realized.

God Realized Is God Demonstrated

Where God is realized, God is demonstrated. If you are called upon for help and sit quietly, patiently, and wait for the spirit of the Lord God to be so consciously upon you that you can say, "Ah, now I feel It. Now I have the assurance of It," your patient or student is healed, relieved, or helped. But if you just repeat the cliché, "Oh, God is everywhere," do not expect any great results.

A healer is a person who has the conscious recognition and realization of God's presence—not merely a person who with his mind declares that God is omnipresent. There must be realization for demonstration. The realized Christ is the demonstrated Christ. The unrealized Christ is the undemonstrated Christ. Whether a person demonstrates the Christ or not, the Christ, the presence of God, is a living reality, but It is of no value to him until It is realized.

The Isness of God

God not only is the creative principle of this entire universe, but God is also the maintaining and sustaining principle, for this universe has been in existence for millions and millions of years, and so it will continue, without any help, advice, or prayers from man. This means that if you have been praying to

God for anything, you have been praying amiss, for God's goodness is by Grace, bestowed without man's praying for it or acquainting God with any need or desire.

Do you not see that God is, whether or not man does anything about it? Do you not see that the function of God takes place whether or not man prays, or even whether man is good or bad? Do you not see that the crops are growing in the "bad countries" as well as in the "good countries," if there are any countries that can be labeled good or bad? Do you not see that this world is a God-governed world without any help at all from man?

God is not a giving God. God's givingness consists in having created this universe and in maintaining and sustaining it. That is God's isness. God is not withholding. In the entire history of the world, God has never withheld anything—not the sun or the stars from shining, not the moon from shedding its glow on the earth and influencing the coming in and the going out of the tides, not the fish in the sea or the birds in the air. These, God has never withheld. The activity of God is, always has been, and ever will be a continuous one without any help from man. To be able to see that will bring about a better understanding of the nature of God. And that will leave only one more step for you.

We Must Establish Ourselves in the Orbit of God

Why, if this is true, have so many of us not benefitted by God's grace? Why have we known periods when good was withheld from us—good health, good supply, good personal relationships, or good national or international relationships? Why has there been so much strife on earth? Why has there been so much strife in individual families, national families, and international families? Why do we have periods of boom and periods of depressions, lack, and limitation?

In the light of what you now know about God and the

increasing knowledge which will be yours as you continue to study and meditate, you will have to admit, "God has had nothing to do with any of these discords, because God's grace is forever flowing. The sun is coming up and the moon is going down; the planets are moving in orderly progression in their orbits. God's universe is intact."

Then whose is the responsibility for the troubles of this world? If it does not lie with God, then it must be with man. If there is lack or limitation in any form, health, wealth, happiness, peace, or joy; we, as individuals are responsible for it and not God. And so we do not have to beg and plead with God. We have to examine ourselves. It all comes back to us: "Ye shall know the truth," and when you know the truth, "the truth shall make you free."

Throughout all time, there have been illumined souls, great lights, who have known the truth that makes for freedom. And what is the truth they have discovered and known? Very simply stated it is that the sins and diseases of earth, the trials and tribulations of the world cannot be laid at God's door. They are not God's fault. God is not responsible for them: man is. These great lights have endeavored to teach man how to restore himself to God's grace, how to get back into God's orbit. This does not mean into God's good will because God does not give his good will and God does not withhold His good will. It means that we must learn how to return to the orbit of God, so that we can receive the grace which is freely flowing from God.

There may be several times during the day when outer things become pressing, and then we have to sit down quietly and realize: "Is it possible that these twenty-four hours can go by without my helping God? Does not God need me to advise Him about these next hours? No, God is forever about His business, so I shall sit here quietly and peacefully and be a beholder of God in action." By this acknowledgment, we have brought ourselves back into the orbit and under the government of God.

There may be another period for self-examination: "Have I been entertaining thoughts of envy, malice, hate, bigotry, bias, resentment, or fear this morning? If so, let me purge myself again. Forgive me, Father. I forgive this universe, and You forgive me as I have forgiven this universe." Again, by this inner purging, we have brought ourselves under spiritual grace.

Another time we may ask ourselves: "What am I doing? Am I accepting two powers? If I am, then, that accounts for my fears, because nobody who believes in only one Power has anything to fear. So, if I have felt any fear this morning or this afternoon, I have forgotten that there is only one Power." This is another way of bringing ourselves into the orbit of God and under his government, and then we experience the grace of living without might and without power, but by His spirit.

As we contemplate the wonders of God, all brought about without any help from man, we come into an awareness of the isness of God and relax in that Isness made manifest as the glories of this universe and as man crowned with glory and honor.

First Develop
Your Consciousness

The degree of consciousness that you develop will determine your outward life—the life of the body, the life of the purse, and the life you experience in your community and family. No one can add to your consciousness more than you permit to be added to it. On the other hand, no one can withhold from you any experience to which your consciousness entitles you because your consciousness is the substance of whatever demonstration in life you make.

That leads to what, at first thought, may seem like a very selfish principle, but one which years from now you will realize is actually the most unselfish principle there is. Remember that the Master told his disciples, "Ye are the light of the world,"[3] a light that cannot be hid. But until you become that light, you have nothing to give the world and nothing with which to benefit the world. The world is full of men who can tell the world how to live, but who cannot demonstrate it even for themselves, much less for others.

Therefore, give up all thought of benefitting or helping the world: give up all thought of healing or teaching truth; give up all thought of blessing mankind. This sounds very selfish, but until you have first learned the truth and practiced and demonstrated it to such an extent that you are the very light of truth, you cannot be of any help even to yourself, let alone to others. Let the world come to you and seek you out only when you have become the light that shines in the darkness.

The Price of Truth

Your function and mine is to share the truth with those who seek it: those who want it, who have earned it, and who are willing to pay the price. Perhaps some of you are wondering why there is or should be a price for truth, and what that price is. The Master said, "Go and sell that thou hast."[4] Dedicate yourself, give of yourself, spend unto your last farthing until you have become the very embodiment of Truth Itself, until you have It, until you are It, until It possesses you, until you live, yet not you, but Christ lives your life.

Then as you rise into that awareness, someone will come to you and say, "I don't know why it is, but I feel comfortable when I am in your presence. May I tell you my troubles?" Outwardly you will be all attention, but inwardly you will be saying, "Thank God, I don't believe it," and just because of your not believing it, he will be benefitted.

Error perpetuates itself until it hits up against a state of consciousness that does not accept it. Then it dies. It is like gossip, rumor, or scandal which travels from one person to another until it reaches one person who scornfully repudiates it as nonsense. Then it comes to an end and dies.

Keep Your Spiritual Life and Experience Secret

As you develop a state of consciousness that does not accept error as a reality, one by one people will come to you, some asking you to pray for them or to heal them, and others telling you that they are comforted by being with you. You will then begin to find that you are a light and a blessing. When you discover that, be even more silent than before. Keep it bottled up within yourself because anything in your life that is sacred is secret. You do not go around telling the sacred things in your experience. Those are the things you keep within yourself.

When you have a spiritual experience and tell it to someone who has not had, or even been interested in having, such an experience, he will most likely exclaim, "Why, that is ridiculous. It could not happen." Therefore, your inner communings, the inner light and revelations that come to you, these are to be kept secret between you and God; and when you begin to commune with God, that is when your deepest sense of secrecy comes to the fore. You bless the outside world, not by divulging what has happened to you, but by your risen state of consciousness. At this moment, dedicate your life to the search for the Holy Grail, and then let your service to God and man come after you have found it.

As long as you are searching for truth, you have not very much to share—certainly not enough spiritual power to heal or comfort the people of the world. All you have is a hope, a hope that you are on the right path, a hope that you have found the right teaching, but you are not yet certain; you have not yet had a revelation from God, saying to you, "This is the way"; or "Now *My* power is upon you, and you are ordained."

Continue searching until you discover your path and until it registers in your consciousness so forcefully that you feel, "I now forsake all others. Now I am wedded. This is my way, and I walk in it. This is my path, the path God has shown me. This is my spiritual home. These are the principles with which I can heal, comfort, and bless." Until that time comes, you have not arrived. Until that time comes, you are still searching to find the way, and it is best that you keep silent and keep secret whatever you are doing.

Work with the Principles to Develop a Healing Consciousness

When the day arrives that you absolutely know that you have found your spiritual path or your particular approach to life, then work with the principles it teaches so that you understand the letter of truth upon which you are building your consciousness.

By that time, you will be having requests for help, and people will be asking you what it is you have and asking questions which you will answer according to the principles of truth which you have accepted. At first they come one by one, and then two by two, and this keeps growing and growing until you find yourself in a ministry. You have not sought the ministry: it has sought you. You were merely the light, and the world beheld that light or some little part of it and found its way to you.

That has been my way of working all over this world. The message is not carried out to the world because the world would not understand. Only those understand who have been given the grace of God to be led to this way.

If you are lifted up, you can draw all men to your state of consciousness and can bring them healing. But if you do not have a healing consciousness, what is the point of wanting to heal? You will not heal. If you do not have a developed consciousness of the spirit of God, what is the use of wanting to bless mankind? You will not bless anyone. This is an important point. With their first smattering of truth, many students want to run out to the world, broadcasting the little they know, ignorantly believing that because of their enthusiasm, they can heal. Enthusiasm is not the healing agency. Only the spirit of God is that. Only a developed spiritual consciousness is that.

Therefore, give your first attention to yourself. Study and practice. If necessary practice every day giving treatments to the cats and dogs and birds around you, thus utilizing every opportunity. Silently and secretly practice by helping members of your family. Silently, secretly, practice, practice until you actually witness fruitage taking place. Then keep doubly silent, until somebody comes to you and asks for help. Then one by one, and two by two, the world will come to you—the world that can receive you.

ACROSS THE DESK

Many persons become frightened at the word, "surrender." It conjures up in their minds a life of asceticism with its badge of sackcloth and ashes. Surrender to the will of God, however, has no such meaning—far from it.

In the Infinite Way surrender is a giving up of personal desires, that the will of God may operate in our experience. It is a surrender of our faith and reliance on the shadow, that desire might be replaced by fulfillment, by that *I* that is come that we might have life and that we might have it more abundantly.

How can we humanly know the joys and glories of that abundant life unless we give up the hopeless and fruitless search for satisfaction outside ourselves and begin to search within where it may be found? How can we know that the abundant life is a life of joy until we gain the conviction of the real nature of God as love, as life, and as infinite wisdom? So we go back to our earlier meditation on the nature of God as love, and as we gain a greater awareness of its meaning, new avenues of fulfillment open up before us, but without human planning or desiring. Things come into our experience we could never have dreamed of, and all through this act of surrender. Try it!

TEACHING THE INFINITE WAY
"Teaching the Principle of Secrecy"

"A teacher must have demonstrated that he has kept himself away from the world, that he has had his periods of inner communion—for weeks, months, years, or decades—and that he has attained the power of Grace, the power of inner communion. That inner communion begins to appear visibly tangible in fulfillment, and yet the principle of secrecy is never forsaken. What takes place within the teacher is his secret. He does not have a 'do-gooder' complex. In fact, he loses all desire to save the world, because he knows that the world cannot be saved. No one can go out and give the Infinite Way to the world. The teacher knows that those of his own household will come to him. The manna he has received from heaven he will gladly share, but he will not share it with the world. He does not go out and tell it to his lawyer, tax man, baker, or plumber.

"The teacher will teach secrecy as a principle to the really dedicated students. He must seize the minutes and finally the hours for that inner contemplation which enables him to arrive at a period of inner response, telling no man what he is doing, not letting it be seen, even by his family. He goes where he can do his praying in secrecy. Then as fulfillment comes on the outer plane, he does not explain or tell about it. He keeps the fingers on the lips.

"Secrecy is the greatest power in the world, and the only time an apparent violation of secrecy is permitted is when a teacher is imparting truth to a student, because in doing that he is imparting it to his own self. If he were to impart this to the human mind, he would be hitting up against a brick wall, and it would bounce back at him like a rubber ball thrown against the wall would bounce back. In imparting truth to the receptive consciousness, however, it does not bounce back because when the student brought himself to the teacher, he was seeking not loaves and fishes, but bread, meat, wine, and water, none of these of a material nature.

"Do not do your benevolences to be seen of men. Make certain that you have no desire that the world know about your contributions, that your right hand knows not what your left hand is doing. It is perfectly all right for the community fund or the Boy Scouts to know that you are a generous giver as long as they do not and you do not make it a matter for the newspapers and public acclaim. Praise that comes to you unsolicited is of a different nature. The Master warned against making a public display of benevolences, just as he warned against praying to be seen of men.

"What I give in benevolence, I am not giving to a person. I am giving to the Christ of my own being. It is something that takes place within me. The Christ knows all, and above all, It would recognize and know hypocrisy. Therefore, the Master says that in praying publicly and in doing benevolence publicly you may gain the praise of men, but you lose God. In other words, you lose this that has taken place within you.

"The teacher should teach students not only the value but the power of secrecy and, eventually, should be able to point out that everything that takes place secretly within becomes known without, whereas if it is advertised, it seldom becomes known because it is not even believed. If I walked up and down the whole world declaring how happy I am, I do not think many people would believe it because they are not inclined to believe words that come out of the mouth. But I think that they feel something in a person's attitude and recognize that he is contented, happy, or successful. Once you have made contact with the Spirit within, you really need nothing of 'man, whose breath is in his nostrils,'[1] least of all his praise.

"Secrecy is the greatest power on earth, and the secret inner communion with the Father is the secret of outer harmony. That is what Infinite Way teachers must impart and reveal. If you were my student and if I were teaching continuously, it would be my function to nag you, to keep at you to have enough periods of inner communion and secrecy until I could see by your outer life that you had in some measure attained.

"Much is taught about secrecy in fraternal orders, but little in religion, although secrecy is one of the principles most emphasized by the Master. 'When thou prayest, enter into thy closet.'[2] The spiritual teacher recognizes the power of secrecy and must teach it as a principle, seeing to it that the serious student works with it until he attains the consciousness of it and how it functions. 'I and my Father are one,'[3] and since I am on the spiritual path, I look to God alone for my experience: for my joy, my success, my supply, my happiness, my home, and for my health. Since I am looking only to God for these, why should I tell anyone anything about them? Do they have anything to do with any other person, or do they have to do only with me and my relationship to God? Therefore, unless I still think that I want something from a person, I will go into the inner sanctuary of my own being, and there tabernacle with God.

"If you really are going to God for your good, for your life eternal, for your harmony, and for your fulfillment, then you must learn to pray in secret. You must learn to enter the temple of your own being. This you can do in church if you like, but sometimes the most effective praying is done at home, in an automobile, or out under a tree, where you are not conscious of other people around you, where you can forget self and surroundings and get inside to the Father within.

"I am not going to God for anything. I am going into the inner sanctuary of my being to commune with God and realize my inner oneness with God. I know that none of this is true in the human picture. It becomes true only if, in my innermost being, I can make that contact with God and live with it. 'Thy Father which seeth in secret shall reward thee openly.'[4] What He sees in secret is shouted from the housetops. But only in one way: by demonstration! The world may say, 'Well, he is pretty happy'; 'He is successful'; 'He is joyous'. But that is the way God proclaims it to the world, and I proclaim nothing further than that—not the how, or the why, or the wherefore. That is my secret business until someone comes and asks, 'Won't you share your bread with me?'

"'Do you mean it? Inner bread, or are you looking for something outside?'

"'Whatever it is you have, I hunger for it.'

"'Good, I will teach you. But again, it will only be between the two of us. This will be our secret. What I teach will not be the affair of the outside world, and how I teach will not be the affair of the outside world. What you learn must not be the affair of the outside world either. This is your secret with God until someone comes to you.'

"You cannot be a teacher until someone comes hungering for what you have. You cannot be a healer until someone asks for what you have, because you cannot go out and tell this to the world. The world has no spiritual discernment, so if you should say, 'I have something with which to heal and I have something to teach,' it would not believe it. So you may as well be still until those ready for the truth come to you.

"The principle is that in the secrecy and silence of my inner being, I and my Father become consciously one. The Father can announce Itself to me. I can receive God: I can hear, feel, taste, touch, smell, or however the awareness may come. This is all I need. What is taking place within me becomes tangible in the outer world as effect, as fulfillment. In the presence of God within me is fulfillment out here."

Joel S. Goldsmith, "The New Teaching,"
1963 Kailua Private Class.

Chapter Seven

A Lesson On Grace

Many persons turn to truth primarily for the purpose of finding a way to solve their human problems and then proceed to measure their spiritual progress by how many problems they do not have. This is a false measuring rod, although there undoubtedly does come a time when the complete absence of problems may mean spiritual demonstration or harmony attained. Jesus attained that after the Crucifixion and the Resurrection. Too many students, however, are trying to attain it before the crucifixion and before the demonstration of resurrection. It cannot be accomplished. It must be understood clearly that the demonstration over the beliefs of what we call the human or carnal mind must be made before complete liberation can be attained. It is always a cause for rejoicing, therefore, when we are presented with problems and are able to resolve them.

There was a time when I dreamed of having $100,000. I wanted that amount because the income from it would make me independent, and then I could be a practitioner without any worries. The day I became a practitioner I had exactly $250 in the world, and no human way of getting any more. That has been my salvation because now when I speak about demonstrating supply, I am not speaking from some textbook I have read or even passed an examination on. I am speaking from the experience of having proved the principle of supply.

When I speak about health, I am not speaking from the pages of a book that I have read. I am speaking out of personal experience. In 1921 I was given three months to live by physicians in St. Luke's Hospital in New York City, and many years later I was given only a few hours to live. So twice I have come back from the experience of imminent death, and both times through spiritual demonstration.

What I have not experienced myself, I have experienced in the lives of my patients and students. Almost every problem of human existence has come to my experience directly or indirectly, and in a great measure these have been met.

When we can prove that disease, lack, bad weather, strikes, and all the other claims of human experience cannot separate us from our spiritual mission, then we have made a step forward, because then we can say, "God must have done this. God must have brought me here. Omnipotence must have proved the non-power of adverse circumstances." Therefore we have a greater degree of faith, a greater degree of confidence, a greater assurance that that same God is always with us.

What Is Spiritual Demonstration?

While we are not primarily interested in human demonstration, in order to demonstrate that the Word becomes flesh, it is necessary to prove in our experience that harmony is the normal and natural state of being, regardless of any human conditions that may claim to be a power to interfere. At this point, however, we need to remind ourselves that we are not on the path of material demonstration but of spiritual realization.

Too often we try to show forth a demonstration so that those around us will be convinced. This is a hopeless task, almost an impossible one. Even the Master did not succeed in that demonstration, so how can we? To begin with, what is the demonstration we wish to make? Our demonstration is the realization of God, the demonstration of spiritual harmony, spiritual life, truth, love, spiritual peace, inner peace, inner oneness and communion with God. But if friends and relatives are not on the spiritual path, how can they be convinced? Could they see the demonstration even if it were made?

Is it not understandable that a spiritual demonstration is visible only to those of spiritual apprehension? Is it not true that in order to recognize the Christ, a person must already have attained a measure of Christhood? Peter alone rose high enough to be able to recognize the truth about the Master when he said, "Thou art the Christ, the Son of the living God."[1] And the Master could answer, "Flesh and blood hath not revealed it unto thee, but my Father which is in heaven."[1] In other words, he was saying, "Your brain, your thinking capacity, or your intellect could never reveal to you that I am the Christ. That is something that only spiritual intuition can bring to you."

Over and over again we have witnessed remarkable spiritual healings only to hear the response, "Oh, nature would have taken care of that," or "They probably weren't as sick as they thought they were," or "The x-ray plates were wrong. There must have been some dust on them that looked like a cancer."

Individual Freedom
Must Be Respected

It is quite proper for spiritual students to offer their friends or relatives a cup of cold water, to recommend that they try spiritual healing or teaching, or offer them a pamphlet or a book. But no one should go further than that. Individual freedom to choose his own method of healing must be respected.

We are living in an age where individual freedom is a most

valuable asset. This inner longing for freedom began centuries and centuries ago, and it came to light at critical times in history: at the time of the Magna Carta; again in the French Revolution; and with the Declaration of Independence and the Constitution of the United States. What were these documents and upheavals except man's drive to be politically, religiously, economically, and socially free? In the past thirty years that drive has suffered a reversal which was predicted by the very men who brought forth the Constitution of the United States. They said that there was an element in freedom that could well destroy it: man's inertia, his unwillingness to fight to protect the freedom that he has.

True, when freedom is taken from a person he will fight to the death to regain it, but while he has it he will be negligent of it. He either will not go to the polls to vote, or he will allow himself to be influenced by anyone with a strong mind and, thereby, ultimately bring to pass what we are witnessing in this age: free countries and free people losing their freedom or having it endangered. So responsible a person as a member of the Supreme Court of the United States has said that our liberties are being taken away from us faster than we were ever able to gain them. And that is because we have not been alert.

Freedom to study and practice any spiritual teaching that we choose is a part of that individual freedom man has struggled to achieve. We cherish the freedom to leave any teaching we choose and seek another. That is our right, but is it not also our relative's right to remain in his orthodoxy or *materia medica* if he so desires? So just as you and I expect and demand for ourselves complete freedom to live and to practice a spiritual teaching, so must we grant to our friends and relatives complete freedom to live the life they desire without interference from us.

It is their right, through love, however, if they say that we are ill, to recommend a favorite doctor or remedy, and it is our right, also, to offer them a spiritual teaching or spiritual help, but we should go no further than that.

Knowledge Must Become Realized Truth

It is claimed that only about 500 or fewer persons out of all the multitudes he healed and fed actually witnessed the Resurrection of Jesus Christ. Why? Because the Resurrection was not something that could be seen with physical eyes. The Resurrection had to be spiritually discerned. Is it not recounted that the Master, walking the earth after the Resurrection, spoke to several people without their recognizing him at first? Why? Their eyes did not see him. Only when he touched them spiritually did they awaken to the fact that they were witnessing this great marvel.

We cannot *know* spiritual truth with our mind, although it can be learned with the mind by reading and study. But that is not really knowing it. The knowing takes place when the intellectual perception has gone a step further and has become spiritual vision. So far as intellectual knowledge is concerned, there is no further place to go in our work. But in spite of the fact that the message is there and students have the tapes, we are going to have to go through this work again, and again, and again, until that knowledge which is in the head becomes knowledge in the heart, or spiritual discernment.

It is absolutely necessary that students live with truth, not only until they know it thoroughly with the mind, but until it has become a part of their very consciousness, until it has become so much a part of them that it is instinctive. Then when they are faced with any phase of discord and inharmony, they will be able to say, "Do not repress it. Do not hold it back, not even that cough. Let it come. It isn't a power. It is not going to disturb or harm you, unless you sit there trying to hold it back believing that it is evil. It isn't evil. So let it come."

The Nature of God-Power

We have heard so much about the power of God in religious literature that the belief became prevalent that God is actually a power to be used against evil. This has resulted in the many forms of prayer in which the power of God is invoked against one's enemies or against disease. Throughout the world, in churches, temples, synagogues, and mosques, millions upon millions of people gather weekly or daily to pray that the power of God come to earth in some manner to destroy national or religious enemies, to destroy disease, or overcome fears.

It is more or less universally believed that the power of God can be invoked, that God is a power over conditions that we do not like, and that man, by prayer, can influence God to annihilate his enemies.

Let it first be understood that God is not a power to be used by man. Let it be clear that God cannot be influenced to do something to our enemies or to our disease, that we cannot invoke God-power at will, that our prayers will not change God's will, God's purpose, God's activity, or God's law. In this way we will stop the vain attempt to reach God for some purpose, regardless of how good that purpose may seem to be.

This is the most important lesson we will ever receive on the spiritual path because it enables us to turn from the Santa Claus concept of God and seek an understanding of the nature of God as God is. In every department of material life, two forces are always opposing each other, good and evil, and always one power is used to overthrow another power.

When men discovered that they could not always rely on one power to destroy another, when it was learned that a power which successfully combated another power today might not do so tomorrow, and when it was realized finally that there are not enough material powers always at hand to destroy the erroneous powers, men sought for something else, something new, something different, something more powerful.

This led to the type of God and prayer we witness on earth today. But this God has not performed according to schedule. Prayer has not succeeded in bringing God down to earth to do man's will. Both this man-created God and the human means of reaching Him through prayer have failed. The troubles of the world are multiplied, even after 5,000 years of invoking Deity to smite our enemies.

The question is: when will man stop this nonsense and begin to know God, whom to know aright is life eternal? And the answer is: when the truth-students of this generation begin to understand God and demonstrate God in their experience. As there was one Moses to free multitudes of Hebrews, one Jesus to found a Christian world based on the understanding of God, so today there must be a handful here and there on the earth, courageous enough to turn away from old, outworn concepts of God and prayer, bold enough to explore new paths leading to God-realization.

Under Grace, There Are No Conflicting Powers

In the material sense of life, there are two opposing forces and there is a continuous reaching for more and greater power to overcome other powers. In the spiritual consciousness of life, there are not two powers: there is just spiritual grace. The spiritual life has no conflicting forces or powers, no greater and no lesser. There is a divine grace governing God's creation. In spiritual wisdom there is no God-power to use, to overcome anything, or to change anyone or any condition. The power of God is a spiritual grace, caring spiritually for God's children.

Under Grace we are in a world where there are not two powers or forces, where there are no conflicts, unless in our minds we create them. Living under Grace, we do not permit our mind to entertain two powers or conflicting forces, lest our mind should create enemies for us. In our spiritual awareness we do not pray to be healed of disease; we do not pray that God do something for us or for ours. We rest in Him, in His grace.

God's grace is ever with us. We need not seek It, strive for It, earn It, or deserve It. It is where we are now. God's rain falls on the just and the unjust. Let us rest back in this Grace, relax and rest in the assurance that there are not two powers or two laws. Only God's law *is* spiritual law. There are no other laws. There is no law of God to overcome material forces or powers. We live and move and have our being in spiritual life and love. God's grace alone feeds, clothes, cares, sustains.

God *is*. But God is not a power over other powers. God *is*. Prayer is not a way of getting God to do our will: prayer is a resting in His grace, a silent communion. It is an attitude of listening through which God speaks to us or reveals His grace in our experience. Only as we surrender the paganistic concept of God as Santa Claus, as an avenging presence, or as a superpower over the world, can we settle back in the assurance of His presence made tangible through Grace. We must release ourselves from the belief of God as power into the awareness of God as love, flowing as Grace.

In a God Created Universe, There Are No Evil Powers

We have lost the God-experience because we have developed a material sense in which we have come either to love, hate, or fear that which is in the manifest realm. Paul called it "the creature"[2] and warned against loving the creature more than the Creator. But he could also have warned against fearing the creature more than trusting the Creator.

We are children of God, spiritual offspring. Then how could there be anything ordained to destroy us, to make us sick, dead, or poor? God never created anything empowered to destroy God's universe, and since God created all that was made and all that God made is good, there is no such thing as a destructive power. There is no such thing as a destructive law. There is no such thing as a devil or satan because there never has existed anything except that which God created.

In the first chapter of Genesis, which is the spiritual version of creation, crops were in the ground before there were seeds; there was light before there was a sun or moon in the sky; and man was given dominion over everything that was in the sky, the earth, and beneath the earth. But in the second chapter of Genesis, there is an entirely different creation from the first. In that creation there had to be material seeds, even a rib. In other words, this world evolved out of a world that was already created.

In the Spiritual Way of Life We Do Not Live By Form or Effect

The materialistic world today operates on the basis that there is so much of everything in the world and so many among whom to divide it. No recognition is given to the fact that there is an invisible universe pouring itself out into visible form, faster even than we can use up what is being created. Spiritual wisdom reveals that we do not live by bread alone; we do not live by what is already created. If the whole world disappeared in one smash, those of us who have learned that we do not live on yesterday's manna would find a whole new world springing up again in the very next minute after the crash. That has always been the way.

In the beginning of the depression during the thirties in the United States, men jumped out of windows and shot themselves because of the disappearance of their money in that panic, as if the printing presses were going to stop running or the intelligence that brought them their money could not bring it back a second time. They had become so fascinated with form that when there was no form to see, they were finished. For them, the world was empty. But those who had the courage to face the situation discovered that the same intelligence that made a man's living one time could make it another time, that the cattle on a thousand hills would be there this year, next year, and the year after. Crops would be grown, more oil would be discovered, more gold, more platinum, and more uranium. For some, fortunes grew faster than they ever had before.

And so it is that in our spiritual life we do not live on yesterday's manna; we do not live on effect. Whether that effect is crops in the ground, fruit on trees, or money in the bank, we do not live on that: we live "by every word that proceedeth out of the mouth of God."[3] We live by every word of truth that we can receive in our consciousness.

If all this world drifted away from us, if our money, our relatives, and our friends disappeared in some holocaust, if we have learned not to fear the creature or unduly love the creature, but to love the Lord our God with all our heart and with all our soul, if we have learned to know that there is a spirit in man, we would not be fazed by any situation in the outer realm. Instead, we would pick ourselves up and start all over again and would rise to greater heights than we ever had before.

Many times in the course of history, world civilizations have been wiped out. But always a remnant remained, a remnant to start the new dispensation, which is always a little further advanced than the former one. True, perhaps in every age there will be periods like our last thirty or forty years when men seemed to go backwards, but they seemed to go backwards only for a very good purpose, that is, that they might lose some of their reliance on outer means, material sense, and develop a greater awareness of their spiritual capacity.

Governments go through terrific trials and ordeals in order that some evil part of their government can be replaced with something higher and something better.

Many persons have either had to lose their health or supply in order to be brought to their knees in humility, where they could say, "Material means have failed me. Is there another way?"

And then God has revealed Himself, and said, "Yes, *I* in the midst of thee am mighty. Why haven't you looked in My direction?"

Every material prop is going to be taken away from man, and he is not going to like it any more than men liked losing their fortunes in the depression. But it is not a question of whether or not we like it. It is that in the end every knee must bend to spiritual grace. In the end everyone has to come to God. It is so ordained.

Mankind has come up from an animalistic state of consciousness and is progressing even though there have been periods of retrogression. And so it is that on this spiritual path, you and I are progressing.

How Problems Help Us on the Path

Problems there must be, because it is these very problems that take from us our reliance on material power, whether it is the power of money, the power of medicine, or the power of government. Each one of us must come to the acknowledgment of God as our government, God as our supply, God as our health, God as the very temple of our bodies. How are we going to do that if we are merely enjoying good health and good supply? Under those circumstances we would be content to rest on our good health and our good supply and we would have no need of God. It is by our problems that we are made to realize that we need Something greater than that which has form.

In what way have we worshiped form? In what way do we still place our reliance on form? In considering that, we begin to perceive why we must rise above the material sense of existence. In the material sense of existence with its two powers, we are always searching for some greater power with which to overcome the discord. In many cases the same mistake was made when individuals came to the mental way of life or the mental sciences. They looked for some thought to hold on to, to overcome some error or discord, always looking to some thing or thought to overcome another thing or thought. But not in spiritual wisdom, not in spiritual consciousness, and certainly not in spiritual healing.

Resting in the One and Only All in All

In spiritual healing and spiritual living, we learn to relax and ask, "Is there any power apart from God? Is there? Is there any power with which God has to contend? Is there any power that God must overcome?" If we persist in this contemplative form of meditation, ultimately we can say, "I know not any. God is supreme, all, infinite. God is one. Besides God there is no power. Besides God there is no law; besides God there is no life; and besides God there is no love." When we come to that realization, we come into the realm of Grace where there are no more battles.

We do not battle people; we do not battle ideologies; we do not battle. We rest as we learn to commune with God, contemplate God, and understand that we live by His grace. Then we rise out of that material sense of existence where there are two conflicting powers—health and disease, sin and purity, discord and harmony—to where there is only One, and *I* am that One.

> *I* in the midst of you am the Presence that goes
> before you to "make the crooked places straight.[4] . . .
> The battle is not yours, but God's. . . . Ye shall not
> need to fight in this battle: set yourselves, stand ye
> still, and see the salvation of the Lord."[5]

This is the state of Grace that is being revealed to us: the battle is not ours. God is the central theme of our existence, and God governs, not by power and not by might. God is Spirit, and He does not overcome. We overcome the belief that there is something to be overcome. We rise above the fear of "the creature," that which has form. To one it is the form of a germ, infection or contagion. Another time it is the fear of a lack or limitation, fear of a strike, a depression, or a war. As long as our trust is in forms, we will be made to fear forms, until we come to the realization, "Form is not power. The creature is not power." Let us not worship the creature more than we worship our Creator. God alone, the Spirit within us, is the all-power.

If we know God, we have demonstrated life eternal, because then we understand God as a divine, eternal, immortal state of Grace, acting through Grace, loving through Grace. No longer will we fear physical might or mental powers, for we will live by Grace. We will not live in an atmosphere where there is a continual warfare between one thing and another, not even a warfare between God and devil. God is so infinite and all, that there is no devil. The devil is absorbed right into God's allness. And just in that way do the so-called sins and diseases of mankind become absorbed, until there is nothing visible left but the body of God: eternal, immortal, and forever and forever.

How the Conviction of One Power Comes

We can take this knowledge and apply it each day as problems arise, until one of these days, bit by bit, the complete conviction of it dawns in us. And then the creature is not a dangerous form any more: it is a companionable form. It was only Adam who named things good and Adam who named things evil. But in and of themselves there never were any evil things and evil beings, never any evil persons. God constitutes individual being. God constitutes your being and my being, his being, her being, and its being. Whether or not they know this truth, the response to us is in accordance with what we know. "Ye shall know the truth, and the truth shall make you free."[6]

If anything has form, even the minute form of an atom, let us not fear it or fear anything that has form, not even a thought. There is not any thing that can disturb or destroy our life since in God-consciousness there are not two powers. There is only one Power: Nothing to be overcome, nothing to be destroyed, nothing to be changed. It is merely that our eyes be opened that we may behold Him as He is, and we will be satisfied with this likeness.

As we look around us, we may see erroneous forms, things

called sin, disease, death, lack, limitation. But be assured that once we have retreated from the belief in two powers, we will no longer behold enemies. They will have destroyed themselves. They will have wiped themselves right off the battlefield the moment we are able to rest in the realization, "Why should I fear any creature? Why should not I love and trust the creative Principle of all creation? Why should I fear that which has form? Did not God create all that was created?"

As we settle back in the assurance that God's grace is our sufficiency in all things, the realization comes:

> Live not by might, nor by power,
> but by My Spirit. Rest back in Me and know
> that I will never leave you, nor forsake you.
> Look unto Me, the kingdom of God within you,
> and be saved. Thou shalt not fear what mortal man
> can do to you. Thou shalt not fear what mortal con-
> ditions can do to you. My ever present Grace is thy
> sufficiency. If you make your bed in hell, I will be
> there. If you make mistakes I will be there.

Let us ponder the great world where we live in which there are no powers external to us. The only power is within us, and it is the grace of God. We need not pray to It for anything. We need not tell It of our needs. It is infinite intelligence; It is divine love. It knows our need before we do, and it is Its good pleasure to give us the kingdom. Let us rest in It, rest in Its grace which is our sufficiency in all things. Let us be beholders and watch God's grace flow as we withdraw from the battle of life, from the struggle to overcome, to destroy, or to change anything.

ACROSS THE DESK

This is the year and this is the month of the 200th anniversary of our Declaration of Independence which has gone down through the years as a statement of man's essential equality and rightful heritage of "liberty and the pursuit of happiness." Even though human birth and this world of appearances may negate that equality, it is an eternal verity because God has planted Itself in the midst of each one of us with Its infinite capacity and potentiality.

The thesis of equality has survived these 200 years, but to far too many, equality is a myth or wishful thinking. Not so to Infinite Way students. It is our privilege and duty to make the dream of the Founding Fathers no longer a dream of visionaries but an actuality. How? Every day, let us have meditation periods in which we recognize God as individual being and each individual as expressing all the divine qualities without limitation. Any barrier to that expression and fulfillment of our divine destiny is but a belief in twoness: a belief in two powers which constitutes the carnal mind, a universal mesmerism. But can the son of God, God individualized, be a victim of the carnal mind or of a universal mesmerism? Impossible!

Our daily realization of these truths will help to lift the unequal burdens of human consciousness and reveal the freedom, expansiveness, and glory of spiritual identity. Can we be that little band of dedicated citizens who can see through the mesmerism of human inequality with its ever present temptation to double-dealing, conniving, corruption, and crime to the eternal freedom, completeness, and perfection of the son of God right here and now and thus make the "noble experiment" no longer an experiment but a realized fact?

TAPE RECORDED EXCERPTS
Prepared by the Editor

In the Infinite Way, the emphasis is never on healing a physical body or on improving some human situation. In fact, any such purpose must be forsaken. Our function in this work is to lift up the son of God in everyone who comes to us. That is why the real healing is revealing the spiritual identity of the individual, and this involves an emptying out process which calls for a "dying" to the personal sense of *I* and a recognition of the *I* that *I Am.*

"As an Empty Vessel"

"You cannot add spirituality to a vessel already full of materiality. . . . Our vessel must be empty of self before it can be filled with the grace of God. . . . Certainly, in its early stages, it may be painful when It is breaking up the humanness in us, when It is breaking up the physical discords in us, when It is destroying in us the wrong moral sense that we carry around at times. Certainly, there will be disturbances in our existence, but we must accept those with gratitude, for it indicates that no longer are these traits, qualities, and conditions lying dormant within us. Now they are being roused up, rooted out, and we will be purified if we are faithful."

Joel S. Goldsmith, "Self-Surrender,"
The 1958 London Open Class.

"Our spiritual goal is not developing a self that has no problems, but 'dying' to the self that has or does not have them, and being reborn of our already perfected Self. . . . You have to go beyond the best humanhood known before you can find spiritual identity. . . . You must think beyond the demonstration of healthy humanhood, wealthy or happy humanhood."

Joel S. Goldsmith, "The Temple Not Made with Hands,"
The 1962 London Special Class.

"'God, . . . destroy my humanhood; destroy the limited sense of myself that I am now entertaining; destroy finiteness in me; destroy the combination of good and evil in me, and consecrate me to your Self. Give me that purity which I had with Thee in the beginning.'

"We are dedicating ourselves to the divine influence that It may enter, permeate our consciousness, and govern us."

Joel S. Goldsmith, "The Dedicated Consciousness,"
The 1964 San Fernando Valley Center Class.

"As long as we are exchanging physical discord for physical harmony, we still have no idea what the kingdom of God is like or what the spiritual riches are like or even spiritual health. We have no idea of it. Just the fact that the heart beats regularly or that the organs function what the world calls normally gives no impression of what spiritual harmony is like, none at all. It is only when we rise above physical harmony that we begin to enter the spiritual realm. . . .

"The nations of the world are seeking God so that they can have more earthly things, better earthly things, so that they can catch larger fish in their nets, bigger fish, better fish. But the basis of our work is 'leave your nets.' The basis of our work is to leave this search for more and better human good and open consciousness to the spiritual realities."

Joel S. Goldsmith, "The Cosmic Law and the Realized Christ,"
The 1955 First Kailua Study Group.

Chapter Eight

Spiritual Supply

The entire subject of supply must be approached from the standpoint, not of your supply or mine, but of what is the principle of supply?

In the spiritual realm we always deal with principles, and when we deal with principles, the truth about any principle is true of any and every individual. The only reason we do not all equally demonstrate a specific principle is that we do not know the truth. We can demonstrate only whatever of truth we know. "Ye shall know the truth, and the truth shall make you free,"[1] but you must know it and I must know it, and any truth that we do not know we cannot expect to demonstrate.

Impersonalizing Supply

In demonstrating supply the first step is to impersonalize it, so that you do not think in terms of "my" supply or "your" supply, because there is no truth about "your" supply or "my" supply. There is only the truth about supply, and this truth is universal. It makes no difference whether it is the financing of our families, our church, or financing a world-wide movement because once this principle is learned, the amount involved is of no importance. It is just as easy to demonstrate a hundred thousand dollars a year as it is one thousand dollars a year, if the principle is known and understood and if there is a legitimate need for the larger amount. Spiritually, no one could demonstrate even one dollar if behind the attempted demonstration there is a wrong motive, a selfish motive, or a destructive one.

It would take many weeks to show you step by step the way in which I learned these principles, but I can give you the principles I have learned and those that I have watched in operation in the financing of my personal needs, those of my family, those of the Infinite Way, and in these thirty years all that I have witnessed in the experience of our students.

The Invisible Supply of a Tree

To begin with, supply is never visible. No one has ever seen supply. All that you can ever see of supply is the effect of supply, but never the supply itself. That, of course, I can explain to you very quickly. As you look at a fruit tree in your garden that is full of fruit, you may believe that that fruit is supply and that that supply is your livelihood. As a matter of fact, that fruit is not supply, never has been, and never can be under any circumstances. It is only the effect of supply, and when you remove the fruit from the tree, whether a wind blows it away, or whether you eat it, sell it, or give it away, you have just as much supply left as when the fruit was on the tree. The proof of that is that in due season there will be another crop there. If the fruit were supply, there would be no place from which a crop could come. A crop has to come from some place, and that some place is the supply.

What is the supply of the fruit then? The invisible life of the tree. The invisible life of the tree enables the roots to draw into themselves all that they require from the ground, from the sunshine, from the rain, or from the dew. All this, going down into the earth, the life of the tree draws into its roots. If there were no life in the tree, the roots would serve no purpose. They could not possibly draw anything into themselves as roots. It is only because the roots have life that they can function and draw to themselves whatever elements or substances they require from the surrounding earth, water, and sunshine.

Because there is life in the tree, whatever is drawn into the roots is transmuted into, let us say, sap. Because there is life in the tree, that sap defies the law of gravity and rises upward through the trunk of the tree, flows out into the branches, and there becomes transmuted again into leaves, buds, flowers, and finally fruit. The trunk of the tree could not do this by itself. It is only because there is life functioning in that tree that the trunk is able to have the sap drawn up into it and then spread out into the branches.

The whole secret of the supply of the tree is the life of the tree, and as long as there is life, the tree will function. Every part of it will function, from the roots right out to the tips of the branches, and there will be fruit. So if you lose a crop, if you sell it, eat it, or give it away, as long as the supply of life is there, another crop will immediately begin to grow and, in its due season, will appear.

Using Wisdom in Operating a Business

If you will apply the principle of the invisible nature of supply to yourself, to your business, or to your spiritual activity, you will realize that money is not supply, nor is the merchandise in your shop supply. Your supply is the life that animates you. In turn, *you* are the life and intelligence of your business. If there were no you, your business would be dead. The merchandise would stay on the shelves, or there would be no merchandise attracted, or the wrong merchandise would be placed there. In other words, it is the life and intelligence that you bring to your business that becomes the substance of your business, and therefore, your life and your intelligence are the supply to that business.

So it can be proved, beyond all question of doubt, that the only success a business has is the life and intelligence of its management or its owner. Your business cannot make money or lose money. Only you can make your business a success by being alive to the truth of the real nature of business.

In every walk of life, regardless of what your seeming income or lack of income may be, you can begin with the realization that money is not supply. *I* am supply. *I,* my life and my intelligence, am the law of supply. God constitutes my life: God constitutes my intelligence; God constitutes my wisdom, and my judgment. Therefore, my life, my mind, my wisdom, my intelligence, my judgment: these are my supply. If I do not have a dollar, as long as I have life, wisdom, intelligence, I will soon have a dollar, and then it will be multiplied. Why? Because supply is invisible, and money, business, and income are the effects of supply.

Supply Cannot Come to You

We go from there to another point, and this is what separates most people from supply. They believe it can come to them from either a human source or a divine source. They believe that supply can come to them through business, through investments, through relatives, through friends, and in this modern day, many persons have accepted the belief that they can get it from their government, as if their government had any money that did not first come from them.

Supply cannot come to you from anywhere, not even from God, for God is not withholding it, and if God is not withholding it, God cannot start it on its way to you. The secret of it is: "Son, thou art ever with me, and all that I have is thine."[2] The sooner you stop looking to God or to persons for money or supply and begin to accept the scriptural revelation, "Son, all that I have is thine," the sooner you will live as a son of God, heir of God, joint-heir to all the heavenly riches. This is true *now.* The life of God is your life; the mind of God is your mind; the wisdom of God is your wisdom; the soul of God is your soul.

There are not two: there is only One, and that One is God. Because of divine sonship, because of your relationship as one with God, all that God is, you are; all that God has, you have; all that the Father has is yours.

I am not talking about money, because God has no money and has no need of money. God has life and is life, and that life is yours. God is mind, and that mind is yours; God is soul, and that soul is yours; God is infinite wisdom, and that wisdom is yours by virtue of oneness. Therefore, in order to show forth the abundance which is rightfully yours, you have to stop looking for it from "man, whose breath is in his nostrils,"[3] stop looking for it from God, and begin to understand that you already have it.

Elijah Fed by a Poor Widow

The example in scripture of Elijah meeting a poor widow and asking her for water and bread might be likened to your asking your practitioner for help on supply, and your practitioner responding, "What have you in the house?" You would probably reply, "If I had anything, I would not be here asking you to help me."

But Elijah knew spiritual wisdom, and out of that spiritual wisdom he insisted that she make him "thereof a little cake first,"[4] after she acknowledged that she had a little oil and a little meal. Imagine your telling your practitioner that you still had five dollars left, and your practitioner then asked you to give it to him! How quickly you would think, "How commercial he is!" As a matter of fact, that is what Elijah did. The poor widow had a little oil and a little meal, and he asked her to "make it up for him."

The woman was trusting, and she made it up into a cake for him, but as she poured, she discovered that the cruse of oil never failed: it just kept on pouring.

Begin To Pour

So a tremendous lesson is learned. There is no use going outside your house, which means your consciousness, for supply. You already have it, and you have to begin to pour it and share it. It may well be that you are down to your last dollar, but that does not mean that you cannot take ten percent of that dollar and give it or share it, for the simple reason that that small percentage is not going to save you in the end anyhow, so you might as well get along with ninety percent of what you have, and either succeed or fail.

You have to find that you do have something in your house, in your consciousness, and whether it is an old pair of shoes in the closet that you are not using anymore, an old suit, an old dress, or loose pennies, you have to begin pouring it. Once you start pouring, you will discover the spiritual principle: it never stops: it never fails.

This was the principle used by Christ Jesus in the multiplying of the loaves and fishes. When the disciple came to him and told him of the multitude waiting to be fed, he also asked, "What have you?" And he received the same answer: "A couple of loaves of bread and a few fish." And "Jesus took the loaves; and when he had given thanks, he distributed to the disciples."[5] This is the same principle as that of Elijah and the widow's cruse of oil.

Tithing as a Spiritual Principle

The secret of supply is, first of all, that supply is invisible; it is spiritual; it is the life of God in you. That is your supply, and it will begin to appear visibly as form only when you begin to pour.

The Hebrews did learn that very early in their experience, and they began the practice of tithing and of giving of the first fruits. As long as they practiced that, they did not know lack or limitation for any lengthy periods. In the depression of the 1930's in the United States, there were not many families that could boast that they went through those ten years without being on the relief rolls or the government rolls at some time or other, but there were certain groups that were never on the relief rolls and knew very little unemployment.

All these groups had one thing in common: they tithed. With some, it was not really a set tithing, but if what they contributed to their church in the course of the year were counted, on the average it would have been much more than ten percent of their income.

A mistake that many people make is to believe that by the act of tithing they ensure their economic security. That is not true. You cannot give ten percent and expect a return of ninety percent. You cannot make a deal with God. It is not that way at all, and that never was the object or goal of tithing. Tithing does not mean giving ten percent to get back something. Tithing means the dedication of a part of one's income to some impersonal cause, and it does not make any difference which cause, as long as it is one of integrity. It is a dedication that enables a person to say, "I unequivocally want to share ten percent of my earnings."

No one who tithes remains at the ten percent level for too long, because it really seems a little bit wicked, after a while, to keep as much as one is keeping. I have known people who have tithed up to eighty percent of their income and known no lack.

Giving to an Impersonal Cause

If you feel that your church or your spiritual activity is serving a useful function on earth and that it is benefitting some people in the world, then how can you help feeling that that is what you want to support so that it can do even greater works. If you have derived a benefit from it, how can you help but feel, "Well, certainly I want someone else, in his time, to derive that same benefit, too."

Though you may not be suffering lack or limitation, some-where in this world there are those who are, and you want to help them. There is no country that we know about that is giving adequate education to its children. There is not a country that has enough schools, enough teachers in the schools, or enough textbooks, or if it has all those, it has not quite the quality of these that it should have. Therefore, what more noble thing is there than contributing to some educational cause that will help some children get more education than otherwise would be the case.

Again, how many underprivileged children are there who never know a summer vacation or a summer camp? What more worthwhile thing is there, if you have a dollar more than you need, to take a dollar or two or ten, even if you have to give up a hairdo, or a haircut, or an extra shirt, and say, "At least through my giving, one child is going to know some sunshine and fresh air."

This cannot be done with the idea of a return. This must be done with the understanding that the Father is forever imparting something to you and you are sharing it. You must let this be poured, not by what you give to your family because that is not unselfish sharing. That is not even giving. Anyone who gives to his family is getting a good return for it. But to give impersonally is pouring oneself out, and more especially if you are obedient to the Master, Christ Jesus, and are willing to give anonymously, so that your fellow man does not see it or know it, so that your fellow man cannot praise you or give you credit for what you are doing.

Let the Father
Reward You Openly

You are told very clearly by the Master that if you give and your fellow man knows about it, you will get some credit from him, but you will lose all the benefits that you would have received from God. That is clearly stated in scripture, and much more clearly stated than I am stating it here to you. If you give benevolence so that your fellow man can see it, you lose whatever benefit might accrue from God.

While it is normal and natural and right to come together to pray, if your praying is limited to your presence in a church, where your neighbors can all see that you are a dutiful citizen, you gain their praise and will be respected by your neighborhood, but you will lose whatever benefit there is from God. You could pray from morning to night and night to morning, and your prayers will not be answered as long as your only prayers are those that you are praying where you can be seen of men.

The prayers that count are the prayers that are uttered when you are in your inner sanctuary, within yourself, in your inner silence, where no man can see or know. Here is the secret of supply. "Thy Father which seeth in secret shall reward thee openly."[6]

Do Not Confuse the Effects of Supply with Supply

It is necessary to turn attention away from thinking of money, merchandise, or crops as supply and realize that these are but the effects of supply. The supply itself is within you. That supply is the life that animates your consciousness, your being, and your body. This life, which is kept secret and sacred within yourself, draws unto you from this world everything that is necessary to your unfoldment. Everything!

It draws everybody to you who can play a part in your demonstration. If you are in business it will draw customers; if you are in the professions it will draw clients; if you are in the healing work it will draw students or patients. It will do all this without working injury to your neighbor, without bankrupting anyone or depriving anyone else, because it is not in the nature of God to benefit one person at the expense of another.

Living the Principle of Supply

Many prayers fail to accomplish their purpose because they are personalized prayers, such as, something for "my business," without a single thought of what is going to happen to the man in the same business next door or across the street. A prayer that would include a person's competitors and everyone in any similar line of work or business would benefit everyone and would be a fruitful prayer.

Realize that supply cannot come to you. It is the life which is in you which is your supply, and it is already there. The way to make it appear visibly is to begin pouring, bring it out into action, and then the flow of "oil" will begin.

Sometimes when writers believe they are barren and there is nothing to write, they discover that if they take pencil, pen, or typewriter, and begin writing and keep writing whatever it is that comes to their mind, before they have gone half a page, they will rip that out and throw it away, and the ideas will begin to flow. All they have to do is let something come out, and before they recognize what has happened, the real stream that they are waiting for will be there.

In my work I go on a platform with no notes and no prepared subject except that I have done my meditation work so that I know that I am an instrument for whatever it is that has brought the Infinite Way into expression, and then I open my mouth and begin to talk. Some students who have been with me for many years tell me that they know exactly what minute the inspiration begins to flow, whether it does when my mouth first opens or whether I just talk for five minutes, and then all of a sudden the inspiration comes. Some of them tell me they can detect that, and I have no doubt that if they are with me long enough they can, because sometimes it does happen that the first moment I am on the platform it does not begin to register, and so I just have to open my mouth and talk until the "cruse of oil" is flowing. Then to my surprise I hear the tape recorder stop and I know sixty or seventy minutes have gone by, and they have all been filled without an interval to interrupt them.

Discovering the Source of Supply

Supply is as impersonal as sunshine or rain. It does not belong to anybody. Supply is not earmarked for anybody, and it does not make any difference what church a person belongs to, what his color or what his creed, or even if he has none, he still has within himself all that the Father has given him. And the Father has given him Himself, therefore everyone has all of this, but only those can bring it into expression who know this truth.

I, the Father within you, is bread, meat, wine, and water. The Father within you is life eternal. The Father within you! This *I* that will never leave you, this *I* that will never forsake you, this *I* that has been with you since before Abraham was and will be with you to the end of the world, this *I* is meat, wine, water, clothing, housing, transportation, and It begins to unfold almost as soon as you know this truth.

It may be that you will have to abide with this truth for days. I have known the day when I did not have ten cents for carfare and had to walk seven miles to get to my office, and that not just for one day. It was during one of those seven-mile walks that I learned this principle. I turned to God and asked Him, "What is wrong? Humanly, I am living a right life. Humanly, I am doing everything that can be expected of me. I do not know of anything more that can be done. I do not mean I am perfect. I mean I am only as perfect as I have the capacity to be. I am not doing anything consciously wrong. What is wrong? What is wrong with this picture?"

Then the Word began to come, "You do not know God. If you knew God, you could never lack."

"But how can that be? Not only am I a student of truth, but I am doing some very good healing work, too, so if I do not know about God, pray tell me what more is there to know?"

The answer came back, "You know a lot *about* God: you do not *know* God."

So I began engaging in an inner contemplation, and I went through all the things that I thought God is. But always the answer came back, "No, God is not mind: that is just an idea in your head. God is not love: that is just a thought in your mind. God is not spirit: you do not even know what spirit is, so if God were spirit you would not know anything about it. God is life? That is only an idea that you are repeating and quoting. You don't know anything!"

"What is God?" and I went through every thought I could think of about God, and all that I got was, "That is another idea in your head. This still is not God."

Eventually I came to the place where It said, "Have you forgotten? *I* in the midst of thee am mighty? *I* am the bread, and the meat, and the wine."

"Yes, that must be God. That is not a word in my head: that is a Selfhood, that is a Being. That is the Being that I am; so my supply is within me, and I have been out here looking for it to come to me from patients, from students, from friends, and all the time I had within me the Source of supply, the Creator of supply, the Fountainhead of supply. I have all of that within me. Now I know why I must let it pour, why it cannot come to me, why it must go out from me!"[7]

Letting Supply Flow

I determined not to keep the first dollar that came in. I would give it away. It was a very hard dollar to give away, but I did. It was not quite certain where the next one was coming from, and I felt that I really should hold on to this one while I had it; but I didn't. I had had my lesson. That first dollar must go. That was the beginning.

It took several days before the supply began to flow, really flow, but then when it did, it began to flow in a way that met my immediate needs, and gradually, over a period of time, paid off all the money that I owed, and from then on, began to be more than I had immediate need for. That was the beginning of my understanding of supply, and that is how the activity of the Infinite Way has been supplied. No one is asked for money, and there are no memberships. It is supplied because I begin each day with whatever I have, and I spend for whatever need there is, and somehow or other, when the year rolls around, all the bills are paid, and on time, and always twelve basketfuls left over to share with others.

Regardless of the state of the finances of some of our students when they first come to the Infinite Way, within two, three, or four years, the situation changes, sometimes little by little and other times in a very startling way. But always after two, three, four, or five years you can see a whole different-appearing set of students than they were when they began, both from the standpoint of physical appearance, economic stability, and in other significant ways.

You owe yourself the opportunity of obeying the teaching of Christ Jesus. You owe yourself the opportunity of proving that all that the Father has is yours, that *I*, within you, is the source of your supply, *I*, the life which is God, *I*, which will never leave you or forsake you. Begin to acknowledge that you have infinity and then begin to pour it. In your pouring, insofar as possible, pour without letting your neighbor know that you are doing it. Pray without letting your neighbor know that you are praying.

You do not have to let anyone know the extent of your benevolences, either philanthropic or religious. You need not let anyone know that, not even the members of your family. You must, if necessary, sacrifice something of yourself so that even your family does not know what you are doing, and they need not know, because neither they nor your neighbor will reward you. But your heavenly Father knows what goes on in secret, and He will reward you openly. What you are doing secretly is being made manifest to those of any discernment, and you are hiding nothing from them.

The spiritual life is a secret way of life as well as a sacred one. In 400,000 miles of traveling that I did in a period of eight years, no one ever knew what my work was except those who were a part of it. As far as the hotels where I stayed and the people I met were concerned I was just another tourist. Religion was not discussed or mentioned. I would never discuss it except with those who are led to me and who have given an indication that they have an interest in it, but it must come from them, not from me. I have learned that nobody is interested in anything that I have discovered unless that interest has developed from within him. I cannot develop it. I cannot even develop it in my relatives. It has to develop within them.

The All-Sufficiency of One Principle

One principle of truth is infinite. One principle of truth includes all the other truths. If you have proved any one of them, you have really proved all of them. If out of all the passages in the New Testament, you can find one passage that you can live with until you demonstrate it, you will have demonstrated the whole New Testament.

In demonstrating health you will demonstrate supply; in demonstrating supply you will demonstrate health; in demonstrating health and supply you will demonstrate companionship and happy human relationships. All these things will be added unto you if you can fulfill the first: "Seek ye first the kingdom of God"[8]—seek this realm of God, seek this truth of God, seek this consciousness of God—and you will have an infinite supply of health, money, opportunity, business, of all the things of God. Acknowledge the infinite nature of your own being by virtue of the grace of God, not by virtue of yourself.

> Of myself I can do nothing; of myself I am nothing.
> But because I am a branch of the Tree of Life, all that

the Tree has is mine, and I can be a whole branch full
of fruit, just so full that it is weighed down—not by
virtue of myself, but by acknowledging that my oneness with God constitutes my oneness with all being,
with all spiritual reality, and with all good.

Then, maintain this silently and sacredly and begin to pour
secretly. Begin to share and to give impersonally. The giving is
not for a return, but out of gratitude that you have discovered
that your supply is infinite and that you already have it. You not
only have a part of supply, you have the whole source of supply.

You do not want to demonstrate supply; you do not want
to demonstrate money: you want to demonstrate the source of
all supply, and that is God. The name of that God is *I,* and that
I is deep down within you. It is something you hold secretly and
sacredly within yourself.

As long as you hold the name of God secretly and sacredly
within yourself and realize that It is the substance of life, the
substance of form, the substance of supply, the substance of
your fruitage, then you can share because it is ever flowing.

ACROSS THE DESK

Perhaps during the course of our experience, we may find
ourselves involved in a court action of some kind. It may be a
situation in which we appear to be the victims of something
beyond our control. How do we approach such a problem from
the standpoint of Infinite Way principles?

Our first step is to turn immediately from the picture to the
kingdom within that the truth of the situation may be revealed.
We release ourselves from outlining the results because we cannot know what a fair judgment should be. Then, from the inner
depths may come the assurance, "God is the judge. God is the
only lawgiver. He alone will save."

This assurance must deepen to a realization that all there is to all parties involved—lawyers, plaintiff, defendant, judge, and jury—is God: God appearing as these.

God is one. The conflict appearing to us is the fabric of illusion. Rather than trying to adjust the illusion, we go to the Source, the One, and release the results into the hands of that One. And what a release that is!

In the realization of oneness, conflict of whatever name or nature dissolves, and justice reigns.

TAPE RECORDED EXCERPTS
Prepared by the Editor

Nuggets

"From the minute we awaken in the morning, we have to embrace God in our consciousness. . . . In everything we do, in every way we do it, we have to acknowledge that we are showing forth God's glory and that everything we do attests to God's presence in us and God's power. The more we acknowledge It consciously, the more we bring It into actual being. . . . Living is shown forth in the intensity of the work we are doing and in the intensity of the joy we find in doing it. Living is not made manifest in idleness or in doing nothing: living is made manifest in activity, and in an activity that we can love and enjoy."

Joel S. Goldsmith, "The Demands of the Spiritual Life,"
The 1961 Seattle Special Class.

"Illumination or enlightenment means to be freed. Freed from what? Freed from the material sense of life. That is the only freedom that you can ever attain: freedom from the material sense of life. What is the material sense of life? It is when your faith, hope, reliance, and ambition are in something external. When you believe that life is dependent on a heart, that is material sense. When you believe that strength is dependent on muscles, that is material sense. When you believe that you live by food alone, that is material sense. . . .

"The freedom of illumination is really a freedom from ignorance, because it is only ignorance that can believe that our life is dependent on something in the external realm, whereas the truth is that our life governs the external realm. . . . Illumination does not take place merely by your hearing these words and saying, 'They sound beautiful, and I hope they are true'; or even, 'No, I think they are true.' Those are only steps leading up to illumination.

"Illumination is when that moment of realization comes. . . . It is the attainment of that Fourth-Dimensional consciousness in which we no longer see materially, hear materially, or believe materially, but in which we see through the appearance, just as we see through the appearance of a mirage on a desert."

Joel S. Goldsmith, "Living In, Through, and By the Spirit," *The 1962 Princess Kaiulani Open Class.*

Chapter Nine

Cast Thy Bread on the Waters

God is spirit, and God is infinite: therefore God is infinite spirit. When you ask God for anything, be sure that what you are asking for is spiritual. The Father does not have meat or groceries: the Father does not have shoes; the Father does not have machinery or money. There are no airplanes and there are no automobiles in the kingdom of heaven, so there is no use praying for them. God has nothing but Spirit to give. So there is no use in going to Spirit or the kingdom of heaven for what does not exist there.

"God is a Spirit: and they that worship him must worship him in spirit and in truth."[1] The Master said, "My kingdom is not of this world."[2] Think of what that means. To go to "My kingdom" for something of this world is an impossibility. If it were possible, if it could be done, if you could pray the Father for shoes or automobiles, why, if you are doing it, are you not getting them?

Seek the Kingdom

There are persons who pray for food, clothing, housing, transportation, and automobiles. In fact, some go a step further and name the kind of an automobile they want. But why are these prayers not being answered? Because God does not answer prayers which ask for material things. But you will have an abundance of things when you stop praying for them or trying to demonstrate them, and begin to pray:

> Father, Your grace is my sufficiency. You know my
> need before I do, and it is Your good pleasure to give
> me the Kingdom. Therefore, I leave myself and my
> needs in Your hands. Give me what You will. Be with
> me as You will. Show me; reveal to me; teach me.

But He stipulates the price: you must seek only the kingdom of God and His righteousness.

God Is Not a Servant

There must be no attempt to use God as a servant, as if He were your messenger whom you are sending out to do your errands. God must not be thought of as a human parent that you can go to, cry, and then have something brought to you. God must be understood as the very life of your being, the very soul of you, the very mind of you, the very intelligence of you. It is egotistical for you to believe that you can tell God something that God does not already know.

You should feel that your God is infinite intelligence, and that He can tell you, but you cannot tell Him. You can become a servant of God, but you can never make God your servant. Those who followed Jesus called him "Master," but he called himself a servant of God, an instrument of God. Do you not remember that he said, "I can of mine own self do nothing. . . . If I bear witness of myself, my witness is not true.[3]. . . My doctrine is not mine, but his that sent me.[4]. . . The Father that dwelleth in me, he doeth the works."[5] This you will discover should you ever attempt to be an instrument for healing.

Effects of Mental Manipulation

In spiritual healing work, there is no projection of thought from the practitioner to the patient. No spiritual practitioner would ever address the consciousness of his patient. As a matter of fact, the repercussions on a practitioner who mentally manipulates his patient can be disastrous. It were far better that he had never been born than that he ever attempted to hold, control, or suggestionize the mind of another.

When anyone tries to dominate another person, physically or mentally, he has set up something within himself to destroy himself. This happened long ago when practitioners, who engaged in mental practice, suggestionized their patients and said, "You, Mary Jones, you are spiritual. You are perfect. You are God's perfect child." They kept that up until by evening they had a bad headache, and eventually the pains became so bad that they had to retire from the practice. The mental pressure they were sending out was coming back to them, as it must. But why must it?

In the consciousness of every pure person, there is a spiritual protective influence, and if anyone, anywhere, under any circumstance, sends out a selfish, personal, sensual, or greedy thought, that thought comes bounding right back to that individual and eventually could have serious effects. Even though a practitioner may have the best of intentions in mentalizing for you, you have a spiritual force within you protecting you from outside domination. Unless you are willing to yield yourself to it, you will never be influenced by outside domination of a physical or mental nature. It will only come back upon the one trying to dominate that which he is trying to send forth to you.

When anyone makes an attempt to enslave, physically or mentally—and I do not mean literally in the sense of making a physical slave of a person—or in any way to dominate or take advantage, be assured that he has set in motion the power that will destroy himself.

In bringing India to its freedom, Gandhi used no power, no armies, and no weapons—nothing but the power of nonresistance. But he understood this principle, and with the power of nonresistance he won freedom for his nation. He knew that if a person stands still, without a physical or mental defense, the purity of his consciousness will cause the mental or physical power to return unto the sender. "There is always some leveling circumstance that puts down the overbearing. . . . Though no checks to a new evil appear, the checks exist, and will appear. . . . The dice of God are always loaded."[6]

To Desire Is To Demonstrate Desire

Your state of consciousness is what governs your life. If you have a materialistic state of consciousness, you will reap materialistically. If you have a mental consciousness, all that you can reap is mentality. But if you have a spiritual consciousness, that is what envelopes you, takes over, and manifests itself in your life. Therefore, if you are praying materialistically, you are most likely going to experience limitation because all matter is a form of limitation. If you pray mentally, which is usually a prayer of seeking something, you will probably get back the nature of your prayer. Therefore, what you get back is a seeking, but not the something.

As long as you have a desire, all you can demonstrate is desire. The more you desire, the more desire you will demonstrate, but never fulfillment. In order to reap fulfillment, you must sow fulfillment. The only righteous prayer is:

> I and the Father are one, and all that the Father has is
> mine. God is fulfilling Himself in me. God is fulfill-
> ing Himself through me. God is fulfilling Himself in
> my experience, and all that the Father is, I am.

This is praying the prayer of fulfillment, and the fruitage must be fulfillment.

Why Desire Is Sin

There is a chapter in *The Infinite Way* called "Infinite Way Wisdoms."[7] These mystical passages were not included in the first edition because it took two years for them to come to me, and they were of such a nature that I felt they would not be understood. So I gave them only to twelve of my students, those whom I thought of as the top twelve. They were permitted to have them for two years. Then, the following year they were added to *The Infinite Way*. In these Wisdoms is the statement:

> "The reason all desire is sin
> is that desire is based on the
> concept of a giving or a withholding God."[8]

Desire is the only sin because desire is an acknowledgment of the absence of God. Desire is a claim that God does not know or does not care. Desire means that you want something you do not have, and God is not giving it to you. The truth is that there is nothing that God has that you do not have, but the trouble is that you are not satisfied with what God has: you want something else. That is a sin.

"Son, thou art ever with me, and all that I have is thine.[9]. . . Your heavenly Father knoweth that ye have need of all these things.[10]. . . It is your Father's good pleasure to give you the kingdom."[11] To desire anything other than that is the sin. When you have God, you have all. When you have Love, Life, Truth, Spirit, Soul, and Substance, how can you possibly want anything more? How can you believe that if the spirit of God is dwelling in you and you are the child of God, joint-heir with Christ in God, that anything will be withheld from you? Can the good things of earth to which you are entitled, the added things, come to you if you set up a barrier to them by desiring, wanting, or trying to demonstrate them?

Turn from the Problem

The same principle applies in spiritual healing work. The more you work trying to get rid of a disease or overcome it, the more acute it becomes. The only way to succeed in spiritual healing work is to turn away from the problem, from the name or the nature of the disease, from any attempt to heal it, get rid of it, overcome it, or even to have a desire to do that, and take the attitude: Thy grace is my sufficiency in all things: physical, mental, moral, and financial. Abiding in the presence of God, the word of God, and the realm of God and ignoring the physical evidences, the problems disappear. The moment you place your mind on them and try to work with them, you are building them up. Strange, but that is the way it is.

If you try to reduce a fever by working on it mentally, you will soon see how it will rise, but if you ignore the fever and abide in the realization of God's grace, the fever is dissolved if that realization is deep enough.

God is spirit! When you go to God, seek anything you want, ask for anything you want, as long as it is not something material. Your prayer will be answered and when it is, it interprets itself on the outer plane as good.

Only the Bread You Put Out Comes Back to You

There is another point, and this is the most difficult point in religion of any kind or in mysticism. It is one that no teacher likes to teach because it usually brings out a very unpleasant reaction from some students, but it is one that eventually has to be learned by the student, whether he has a revelation within himself or whether his teacher is willing to risk crucifixion of one sort or another to teach it. Everyone will eventually have to learn that there is only one reason for lack of any kind. You may think there are a thousand reasons, but there is only one, and that one is withholding. It is hard medicine to teach that everyone who lacks is withholding, but let the lightning strike where it may. Supply can come only through giving. The bread that you cast on the water is the bread that comes to you, and the bread that you do not cast on the water cannot come back to you because you have not placed it there. There is a law of God that does not permit you to have the bread that the other person has cast on the water. That bread is earmarked for him

If you are not forgiven for your sins of omission or commission, do not blame God and do not blame those who are not forgiving you. It is your fault because you are not forgiving. You are holding in your consciousness condemnation, criticism, judgment, a hope for punishment, an unforgiveness, and it does not matter whether it is toward an individual, a group, a nation, a religion, or a race. If you search your consciousness, you will find that if you are not forgiven and are being held in any condemnation, it is only because you are holding someone in unforgiveness. It is a law, and there is no use arguing with a teacher about it. It is a law.

If you lack companionship, it is nobody's fault but yours. When students ask, "Won't you pray for me or work for me for companionship," I have only one answer. "You do not want companionship. You want a companion, and I am not in the business of demonstrating companions, because sometimes they backfire."

If you want companionship, your whole being embodies it, so go out and be a companion by expressing companionship. If there is no human being with whom to express companionship, go into the park and express companionship with the birds; go down to the edge of the water and companion with the fish; go out in the garden and companion with the flowers. But express companionship, express love. It will not be long before you will find yourself with a companion, and with one that will not backfire, because you will have brought back to yourself exactly what you put out: companionship, pure, good, unselfish companionship.

Everyone Has Something To Give

There never has been an excuse for continued poverty, for lack or limitation. Look out at this world and see how much wealth there is on every hand. Many persons do not think so, but there is only one reason they are not expressing abundance. They are not giving enough, or they would be partaking of that wealth because nothing can be withheld from those who give.

Lack or limitation is the experience of those who for one reason or another withhold or who accept the belief that they have nothing to give. There is no one who has nothing to give. Everybody can give forgiveness; everybody can give companionship; everybody can give some unselfed service. I do not mean service to your family. There is nothing unselfed or giving about that. That is personal and selfish, for your own good. I am talking about impersonal giving, impersonal service.

With the exception of those who have been hospitalized with a long costly illness, there is no one in the world who does not have a few pennies and who cannot begin to give pennies. In the kingdom of God it is not known whether you give six-pence or six thousand. All that is known is that there is a giving movement going out from the center of your being, but how many pennies, dollars, or pounds given is never seen or known. There is no such things as an account book in the kingdom of heaven.

Poverty Is No Indication of Spirituality

Lack and limitation are unnatural. Long ago it was believed by many persons that if a person was engaged in spiritual work or church work, he should be poverty-stricken, that it was a great honor to be poor. Of course, that did not apply to the church that employed those who were to remain poor. The church could accumulate all the millions and billions on earth and squander them in edifices, stained glass windows, and golden statues, but the spiritual worker or the minister in the church was supposed to be proud to be poor. The laymen who did the hard work in the edifice were to get nothing because they were supposed to get their reward in heaven. That may be a good way to obtain free labor, but it certainly is not spiritual.

To have the abundance of God is spiritual, and if it is spiritual for the businessman and businesswoman to be prosperous, it is even more spiritual for the spiritual worker to be prosperous because he is giving more, sacrificing more, and devoting himself more to the things of the Spirit. The person with a developed spiritual consciousness will never be found squandering that abundance in idle luxury: it will always be used for some worthwhile or charitable purpose.

The point I am trying to make is that prosperity is the natural state of mankind. It is intended that everybody be infinitely prosperous. You cannot count the blades of grass; you cannot count the apples, oranges, peaches, pears, and plums in the world. You cannot count the amount of gold in the earth, the diamonds, platinum, and uranium. You cannot count the wealth in the sea.

Limitation is no part of God's plan. The ocean is full of water and now there is a way of extracting the salt and making the water fresh, so there will be more than enough water for irrigation purposes. In one way or another, it is being proved that abundance is God's intent for His people, and if you are not enjoying abundance, search yourself and see where and how you are violating the laws of God.

Never Seek a Return for What You Do

Experience has taught that the secret of limitation is withholding and the secret of abundance is giving. But it must be understood that you are never giving anything of yourself, for if you think you are, you will impoverish yourself. You came into this world with nothing, and whatever comes to you comes from God, and whatever you have to give, share, and pour out is from God's storehouse, not from yours! Once you begin to perceive this, you will never be satisfied to tithe merely ten percent. It will increase to fifteen percent, twenty, and twenty-five percent, until the day comes, as it has already come in the experience of some persons, that you may be tithing eighty percent.

God's law is giving; God's law is outpouring; God's law is expressing. You are violating God's law when you fail to do that. I am not referring only to money. Money is but one of the facets. Pour out forgiveness; pour out understanding, cooperation and, above all, be sure that you are not seeking to get something.

You have to learn to do whatever you are doing without ever entertaining the thought of a return. In marriage a husband usually contributes one thing and a wife some other thing. It is a mutual giving. Everyone has a different idea of the value of what is given so it does not always work out. It may be that a wife gives eighty percent and her husband twenty percent, but the husband feels that he is giving eighty and the wife is giving twenty because there is no way of putting a market value on the services given by each one.

But what happens in a home when a man does all that he is supposed to do without entertaining the idea that he has something coming to him for what he does. In other words, what he does, he does because he is a husband or a father, and that is his joy. His wife, too, would feel that whatever she is doing, she is not doing for a return or for a living, but because she is a wife or a mother, and therefore, it is her privilege to do it.

The best example of this is spiritual work. There is no real spiritual leader who does whatever he is doing to get something because there is no return that anyone can make to him. A spiritual leader has already found his home in God and, therefore, whatever he wants, he gets from God. There is nothing that anybody can give him. He does not even care whether he gets thanks because what a spiritual leader is doing is not for anyone else's sake. It is for the sake of his own self-expression. He has to do it. He would have to do it if he had no audience or no congregation: he would have to go down to the lake and talk to the fish; he would have to go out to the park and talk to the birds. He would have to express himself because that is his nature. He is filled with God, and he must unburden. I have never known a real spiritual teacher who was interested in getting anyone's thanks or reward. He was there for one purpose: to be used to pour out what he had realized.

If you are in business solely to make money, you are going to have a very hard life, even if you are very successful. When you are in business with the idea, "This is the work I love, and I am going to put my best into it and give the best that is in me," the profits come in. It is only when an individual is in business with his eyes always on the cash register that he can get himself into trouble. So it is in the home, too.

Let the Gift of God Express Through You

Every individual has a mode of self-expression, either as a perfect teacher, a painter, sculptor, carpenter, or a perfect father, a perfect mother, or a perfect housekeeper. Everyone has within himself a capacity for self-expression which removes him from competition.

Whether it is a stenographer, a secretary, or a bookkeeper, every individual in the world has a form of self-expression. If a person is merely typing or keeping books to earn a livelihood, then, of course, he is like every other typist or bookkeeper, in fact, like so many bookkeeping machines: they look alike and act alike. But when a person has in him the idea of expression and of perfection, he is individual in his secretarial or bookkeeping work. That is the difference between poor bookkeepers and good bookkeepers. That is the difference between good accountants and poor accountants, well-paid accountants and underpaid accountants. One is putting himself into his work as a form of self-expression, the other is just doing a job.

Whether you are a wife or a husband, an employer or employee, a neighbor or friend, whatever you are doing should be thought of as a mode of expressing yourself, showing forth your inner nature.

Each one of us has a gift of God. We were not created in herds. Each person was individually conceived and born. It is only man himself that puts himself into herds and ghettos. God does not. God created each person separate and distinct, and each one with a talent, a gift, or some means of self-expression, and when he seeks to express that, he is giving of himself and his talents, and there is no way then to withhold the flood of supply that will return to him.

It is not easy to tell persons who are accustomed to believing that they have an insufficiency that it is their belief that perpetuates the insufficiency, because they have all that God has. Let there be no mistake about that. Everybody has everything that God has, and they never will have more and they never will have less. But neither will they ever have it in external expression until they begin to pour it. Begin with what you have.

Spiritual Living

The one thing you have to do in order to demonstrate the life more abundant is to pour, and pour, and pour, and then you will discover, not merely the principle of supply, but the principle of spiritual living. There is no way to find your life eternal except by giving your life. What you do not give, you will not have. But what you give, even if it is your life, you have, pressed down and running over.

Those who can show forth to you in their spiritual life that they have a lifetime of giving, giving, giving: pouring, pouring, pouring, could also show you that they *have*. Usually they have relative comfort; they have a home; they have few worries; and they have little fear.

When their time comes to make the transition to a higher form of activity, they will go without fear, without holding on to yesterday's manna, without holding on to yesterday's body. Why? Because they have learned that neither life nor death can separate them from the love of God, so whether they live on this plane or whether they live on that plane is a matter of utter indifference to them, because wherever they live, they will be about their Father's business.

Do you see why a lesson like this is difficult? It resolves itself into this truth: God is not responsible for your sins or your diseases, for your lack or your limitation. God has placed an infinite abundance in this world, even of the things of this world, and He has not put anybody's name on them. Not only that, but every year there are new crops; every year there are new opportunities. If you are not receiving what is your due as a child of God, it is because you have not yet become a child of God.

How did Jesus tell you to become a child of God? "Love your enemies, bless them that curse you, do good to them that hate you, and pray for them which despitefully use you, and persecute you; that ye may be the children of your Father which is in heaven."[12] That is the formula that he gave. That does not mean you are not to pray for your friends: it merely means that is not where you derive your reward. Your reward, your divine sonship, comes in praying for your enemy, praying in secret, and giving your alms secretly.

The whole teaching of Christ Jesus is that it is up to you. "O, Jerusalem," he says, "Jerusalem, . . . how often would I have gathered thy children together, even as a hen gathereth her chickens under her wings, and ye would not!"[13]

It is up to you whether you know the truth that makes you free. It is up to you whether you want to pray for your enemies and become children of God. It is up to you whether you want to give alms secretly and sacredly. It is up to you whether you want to love your neighbor as yourself. Jesus cannot make you do it, or you would all be doing it. He can merely tell you what will get you into the kingdom of God. He can be the way-shower and show that his life was successful, harmonious, and abundant. Even in giving his life, he could give it without any fear of death, because he knew the secret of immortality, and he knew that if he gave up his human sense of life he would take on the next life.

What you put into this life is what you will take out. What you put into your spiritual practice is what you will take out. What you give and cast on the water of the bread of life is what is going to come back to you, pressed down and running over.

TAPE RECORDED EXCERPTS
Prepared by the Editor

As the excerpts below indicate, almost every problem we encounter involves some claim of material law: laws of disease, economic laws, laws of weather or climate, laws of cause and effect. It is this material sense of law, which in the consciousness of Spirit as the all-in-all and therefore as the only law, must be recognized as non-power and inoperative. Let us see through the material sense of law and gain a deeper awareness of the nature of spiritual law, governing all and maintaining all according to divine order and harmony.

"Law"

"We have many kinds of law: material laws, mental laws, legal laws, economic laws, karmic laws. Are these law? Only in the absence of truth do these operate as law. They are actually universal beliefs, and in the presence of truth, none of these can operate. Why? God is the only law-giver; therefore, the only law that is must emanate from God. . . .

"If a law can be good and evil or if it can produce good and evil, it is not of God and it is not a law. Why? Because God is infi-

nite good and in Him there is no evil; there are no pairs of oppo-
sites. Evil can never come forth from God, for God is eternal life.
If any evil came forth from God, it would destroy that life. It
would destroy God and therefore it would destroy all that is. . . .
"Only that is law which results in divine harmony or good.
Legal law can be good and it can be bad. Material law can be
used for good, and it can be used for evil. Mental law can be
used for good, and it can be used for evil. Any kind of law that
you can think of, with the exception of spiritual law, has the
potentialities of either good or evil, or of both good and evil.
Therefore, none of these can be law. Only the law of God is law,
and the law of God is life eternal, life immortal, life harmonious, infinite abundance. . . .
"At every point of your human existence you are being faced
with law. . . . It is up to you consciously to know that only the
law of God is law, that only spiritual law is law, that only spiritual law is power. Therefore there is no power in material law,
mental law, hereditary law, or any other law that you can think
of. If it has the possibility of good and evil, it is not of God. . . .
God is the only law-giver; therefore, spiritual law must be the
only presence, the only power, the only reality, the only cause."

Joel S. Goldsmith, "Specific Principles and Application,"
The 1959 Manchester Closed Class.

"When there is restricted inspiration, when there is a
restricted supply of anything—health, money, opportunity—
always remember this: some universal law is operating. . . . Your
patients are not suffering from any fault of their own. . . .
Regardless of what they do, there is an impulsion from the universal. . . . If you divide us up into separate people, and then try
mentally to improve us, you will not get very far. . . .
"There is a way in which you can free people of their discords. . . . It is by turning away from them and recognizing that
this is material law, and it is not power. . . . It is not law; it is not

a cause; it is not power. Why? . . . The only law is Spirit. Mind is not power except on the level of belief. . . . The power is within you, and it does not operate through conscious thought. It only operates when conscious thought has stopped."

Joel S. Goldsmith, "The Law of Moses: The Grace of Christ," *The 1956 Second Steinway Hall Practitioner's Class.*

"Every single spiritual demonstration is an annulling of a physical or mental law. . . . It is annulling or wiping out the operation of physical or mental law. It is lifting you into a realm of consciousness where the particular physical or mental law from which you are suffering no longer operates. To be a healer, it is necessary to dwell in the secret place of the most High, to dwell in that consciousness where physical and mental laws are not operating. This is prayer."

Joel S. Goldsmith, "Self-Purification," *The 1959 Hawaiian Village Closed Class.*

"God is the law-giver, but God is also the law. Why? You cannot separate God from Its creation, so God must be the law-giver. . . . If there is only one law, then there are no laws to fear, whether they are laws of heredity, medical laws, physical laws, or material laws. There is only one law if God is the law-giver, and that law is Spirit. As we live with that truth and hold to the truth that God is Spirit, and therefore, the only law is spiritual law, we will not fear mortal laws, material laws, and ultimately we will see that they are only laws insofar as we accept them."

Joel S. Goldsmith, "The Principle of Our Work," *The 1954 Honolulu Lecture Series.*

Chapter Ten

The New Dispensation

The only place man has to go for anything is to the consciousness of his own being. The reason is that God is consciousness, infinite consciousness, and that Consciousness is the consciousness of individual man: yours and mine, saint and sinner, anywhere, any time.

Some few have learned to go to the kingdom of God within themselves, not for things but for spiritual grace, for the things of God, for the kingdom of God. And they have found their peace, not the peace found in the things of the world or the peace that you can find on earth.

The Infinite Way has revealed that God is consciousness, that Consciousness is the substance of all form, and that this infinite consciousness is your individual consciousness. You do not have a piece of It: you have all of It. The fact that you do not draw forth all of It means that you draw forth only enough to satisfy your immediate needs.

Meditation Reveals Infinity

When you know this, you will understand why meditation as taught in the Infinite Way will have to be introduced to the peoples of the Eastern World. It is true that meditation has always been a way of life in the East but the people there have not known the function of meditation. Most of them do not know that God constitutes individual consciousness and that the purpose of meditation is to go within to open out a way for Infinity to flow forth from within, and that it must not be looked upon as merely a religious practice or discipline. It must be looked upon as the most practical step toward harmony.

If you are ever to know mental, physical, spiritual, economic harmony and freedom, even political freedom, you will know it only by drawing it forth from within your own consciousness. You must not think for a minute that there is going to be a government of men anywhere that will be dedicated solely to the interests of the people of the world so that they will receive abundance, equality, justice, and peace on earth. True, there will be an individual here and there dedicated to freedom for all people, but he will not succeed too well in a world of self-serving politicians. The freedom that you seek—equality, justice, and peace—must flow out from your consciousness.

In proportion as you succeed in drawing forth some measure of what the world recognizes as good, in that degree will you have the capacity to teach others to draw this forth from within themselves. Then you will be able to help those who are led to you by virtue of their being of your household. This does not mean that you can run over to Washington, D.C., to Downing Street, or to the doctors in the hospitals to try to teach them. It means that you must sit in your homes until those are led to you who by Grace have the spiritual capacity to receive what you have to give. But then if they do not have the receptivity to want what you have to give, if their mind is set on the silver and gold, or on things, they will miss the way.

What Is Spiritual Consciousness?

To understand what constitutes spiritual consciousness, you

begin with the principle that God constitutes individual consciousness, but superimposed upon that consciousness is the human mentality or human intellect which has been taught through the ages to accept two powers, two laws, two selves: myself and yourself which hide the God-consciousness which is ours.

As human beings we have no access to God-consciousness, and it is for this reason that as human beings anything can happen to us, and most things do: sin, disease, false appetites, war, slavery, imposition, injustice. Anything and everything can happen to the human race because it has no access to the divine consciousness which all the time is the real consciousness of mankind.

The spiritual consciousness which is the healer is your consciousness in the degree that it has become awake to the errors of the human mind and has come to know that there is not God *and* man. God is manifested *as* man. As you realize more and more clearly that you are one with the Father and that all the Father has is yours, you are building your consciousness of the real Self. You are "dying" to all that constitutes human beliefs and being reborn into your original pure state of Christ-consciousness.

Awakening to Spiritual Consciousness

That Christ-consciousness knows: "I am the bread, the meat, the wine, and the water: I have meat the world knows not of. I have hidden manna." In that one second of knowing, you have "died" to that part of humanhood which believes that you must fight, struggle, or steal to earn a living. That degree of humanhood has left you, and you can rest in the consciousness that says, "I have spiritual bread, meat, wine, and water. I have even the power of resurrection within me." What a release it is not to have to go to God for these things, nor to man, but to awaken to the realization: "I, in my *I*-ness, embody all."

In your humanhood you believe in two powers, the power of health and the power of sickness, but when you grasp the principle of one power, you have died to another part of your humanness, and you do not then even need God to get health for you, since there is no power of illness or no law of ill health. Is it not clear that in that awareness you have died to a part of humanness and have been reborn into some measure of spiritual consciousness?

In humanhood you have been taught that good people receive rewards and bad people punishment, and therefore, when people come with sin, disease, and poverty, your natural inclination is to think that they are being punished or that they are getting what is coming to them. When you realize that God neither punishes nor rewards, that God neither gives nor withholds, you have been reborn into some measure of spiritual consciousness, the Christ-consciousness that does not judge, criticize, or condemn.

In your humanhood, you believe that your enemies always deserve what they get, but no one can expect to be a practitioner or teacher with that kind of consciousness. The practitioner or teacher has to realize constantly the spiritual identity of those looked upon as enemies and the fact that the errors that make them his enemies are all tied up in this mortal illusion of a belief in two powers. To hold a human being in judgment is human consciousness. There is no healing in it. Only as human consciousness is overcome—human qualities, human judgments, human beliefs, human powers—are you reborn into spiritual consciousness.

When a person reaches out to a practitioner for help, he is not touching anybody who is criticizing, judging, or condemning him; he is not even touching a consciousness that believes he is sick; he is not touching a consciousness that believes there are two powers. He is touching divine consciousness.

No one can be a teacher or practitioner in the Infinite Way and go on living according to human standards. He has to develop the consciousness that does not fight evil, that does not judge it, and does not seek to punish it. He has to develop the consciousness that recognizes not only that he and the Father are one, but that you and I are that same one, because there is only one *I,* one Selfhood. But repeating those words is merely paying lip service to the principles. Without some measure of understanding and realization of the principles, there will be no healing consciousness.

This is the goal, and in proportion as you attain this goal, do you become a teacher or practitioner, even though you may not at any time have reached the full measure of manhood in Christ Jesus. Whether you ever will on this plane or not, I do not know, but that is not too important. The important thing is that each day you live up to as much as you can understand and realize, and make no pretensions that you have gone beyond that. It is important not to assume a consciousness you have not attained.

How Long Does the "Dying" Daily Process Continue?

I never ask spiritual perfection of our students. Heaven forbid that I should expect it of them, knowing that I myself have not attained it! But I am grateful for every sign they give me that they are progressing spiritually and dying daily.

How long should that dying go on? The Bible does not state how long it will take; it just says "daily." Daily could go on forever, and perhaps there is a dying daily forever. It may be that no one ever does attain the fullness. But do not worry about how far you are from the full stature of manhood in Christ Jesus; be grateful that you have been given some measure of spiritual light and grace, and that you are some degree further along the path of dying daily and being reborn. Keep it up each day, so that each day you die to some measure of human belief, and each day you are reborn to some activity of spiritual awareness.

The goal of the Infinite Way is to bring the student to the attainment of Christ-consciousness or to that "mind. . . which was also in Christ Jesus."[1] It is that state of consciousness which is of "purer eyes than to behold evil, and canst not look on iniquity"[2] and which, therefore, gives no power to the world of effect. It is the state of consciousness that dissolves every material or mental appearance upon contact, thereby revealing the spiritual presence which is the reality and is omnipresent, even though humanly seen "through a glass, darkly."[3]

The message of the Infinite Way, as it has been given to me and as I have been instructed to introduce it into human consciousness begins with a metaphysics and leads up to the mystical. I say *a* metaphysics because there are several approaches to metaphysics: some completely mental, some partly mental and partly spiritual, and some primarily spiritual with something of the mental. The Infinite Way is the mystical way, which takes the student beyond metaphysics.

Again I remind you that the wisdom of God cannot be imparted to or through or by the human mind. Teachers of the Infinite Way must have risen to some measure of spiritual consciousness or they will soon discover that they cannot teach, impart, reveal, and uplift because, regardless of how well they may know the message of the Infinite Way and its principles, there is no spiritual power until they have been lifted above knowing to being, and being is living without taking thought.

It has been revealed to me that a spiritual or mystical message such as Christ Jesus gave cannot be given to the multitudes: to sick people seeking to be well, poor people seeking to be rich, or unhappy people seeking to be happy. The fact that their mind is centered on the attainment of the things of this world indicates that they are still in the material sense of life and could not receive the wisdom of God even if the teacher had the consciousness to impart it. But if he is in that state of consciousness in which his concern is primarily for the attainment of physical health, supply, and happiness, he could not possibly impart spiritual wisdom because he would have none to impart, nor would he have the consciousness which could receive it from God.

Let us assume, however, that you have demonstrated by

your healing works that you have some measure of that mind that was in Christ Jesus, spiritual consciousness, and that through meditation you are receiving impartations of spiritual wisdom and can impart them. Through my experience, you must know that "the natural man receiveth not the things of the spirit of God,"[4] that you must begin to lead your patients and students up through metaphysics to the mystical consciousness, and that the metaphysics you impart must be the metaphysics embodied in the message of the Infinite Way, *and no other.*

Two cardinal principles of the metaphysics of the Infinite Way are that thought is not power and that the human mind is not power. The human mind is an avenue of awareness. What the world calls the carnal mind, or the belief in two powers, is not power. This principle eventually leads the student to that state of consciousness which recognizes that karmic law itself is not power, since in the presence of the Christ, which is your state of consciousness if you have attained it, there are no other powers. Even Pilate, with all his temporal power, could not be a power; paralysis, with all its claim to power, cannot be a power. Nothing of the nature of matter or mind can be a power in the presence of your consciousness when your consciousness is attuned to the Infinite and is receiving impartations of the Spirit, which really means divine grace.

Becoming an Angel in the Household of God

Every impartation of the Spirit comes as an act of Grace. It is not something earned or deserved: it is not something you are entitled to as a human being, because your humanhood deserves nothing from God, and your humanhood must "die" before your spiritual nature can be revealed and before you can be the recipient of God's grace. God's grace is given only to the children of God, His angels, as a divine inheritance.

Right here is a good place to remind you that there is only one way in which you can become a child of God, an angel of the household of God, and that is in the degree in which you go to God without a desire, a wish, a hope, or a need. You are one of God's angels in the degree you can enter meditation, not with some thought that perhaps you will be able to stop the next war, the next tidal wave, or the next massacre over the weekend holiday on the highways, but when you can ignore every human appearance and seek only an inner communion with the Spirit, that the spirit of God may bear witness with your spirit, and reveal, not a pleasant human world, with all its evils gone, but the kingdom of God on earth, a universe, not of good people, healthy people, and wealthy people, but a universe of spiritually minded people too pure to behold or indulge in iniquity.

Then, as a teacher, you must remember that your function is to lift up the student to that state of consciousness. How are you to do this? God has revealed to me the how and the way for us at this time, is to teach thoroughly the metaphysics of the Infinite Way so that step by step the student can lose his fear of the power of thought, the power of mind, the power of karmic law, the power of germs, the power of accidents, the power of persons; in other words, gradually learn to lose his fear of mind and matter. This is a metaphysical process, and it is attained by the study and the practice of the principles which are embodied in the message of the Infinite Way.

The Mystical Way: Letting Love Live Your Life

You could never bring a student into harmonious relationships, even with the members of his own family, much less the family of nations, unless you can reveal that there is but one Selfhood and that anything you have done of evil to any person you have done unto your Self, which is the Self of the Christ, and the punishment would be in having outraged the Christ. Inasmuch as you have done good unto "the least of these my brethren,"[5] you have done it unto your Self, because the Self of you is the Christ, and the Self of "the least of these" is the Christ.

Therefore, in serving man do you not see that you are serving the Christ? In serving the Christ you are really serving your Self. An injury done to another is an injury done to your Self, and a good done to another is a good done to your Self. This is the basis of karmic law. So to refrain from both good and evil through an understanding of one Selfhood breaks karmic law. Then there is no evil to return to you and no good to return to you: you yourself are the embodiment of the infinity of good.

The student comes to that consciousness through an understanding of the letter of the message and especially through the practice of it. The practice begins inside the home where you are naturally the most impatient. Those who are closest to you are the ones who arouse in you the greatest irritation. It is there that the appearance of two or more separate selves is thrust at you day after day. Humanly the twain will never be one, unless you can begin to perceive, inside your household, that those of your household are you, and you are they, and you are all one. Then you mold your actions so that insofar as possible you are treating each one in the household as you would wish to be treated. This is the discipline that exists in metaphysics.

In the mystical life none of this exists. In the mystical way of life, love is living my life, not the personal sense of "I." You have often heard me say that I do not know what it means to be spiritual; I do not know what it means to be good; I do not know what it means to be benevolent, because I am none of those things. I am witnessing these activities as they flow through me, and I recognize that they never did belong to Joel, therefore, they must be God's grace flowing through him. In that way, then, I am creating neither good karma nor evil karma; I am being, and I am letting God be "me."

From the Law to Grace

Do not expect to find this attitude in your students except in proportion as they take these principles into consciousness, practice them, and above all, practice meditation, because it is not in a mental exercise or in the doing of these things that they attain their spiritual growth.

The Hebrews of old believed that if they obeyed the Ten Commandments they would be good human beings and that would entitle them to heaven. Christians adopted the Ten Commandments and added to them the Sermon on the Mount, believing that if a person loved his neighbor as himself, if he did unto others as he would have them do unto him, this would make him spiritual and good and he would attain heaven. This is far from true. The practice of the Ten Commandments, the Sermon on the Mount, and the principles of the Infinite Way will make a person a very admirable human being, one of whom his family, his nation, and the world can be proud. But it will not get him into heaven.

Only through meditation does a person open his consciousness to the Infinite Invisible, to that which causes him to "die," not only to being a bad human being, but even to being a good human being. As a matter of fact, meditation makes a person transcend human wisdom, because if he has opened a pathway to the Infinite Invisible, through meditation he will receive a knowledge and a wisdom far greater than can be found in books. Books reveal only what is known up to this moment. They cannot reveal what is going to be discovered tomorrow. The discoveries of tomorrow must come out of infinite consciousness, and they can come only to those with the listening ear who hear the Voice, those who, through meditation, are receiving Grace.

Becoming Christed by the Grace of God

Far too many students are trying to become all of the Christ tomorrow or next year, and since they are doomed to failure, why not instruct them that they become Christed only by the grace of God. There is a sufficiency of Grace to bring to them the measure of growth to which they can be receptive at the moment. Each meditation enables a student to receive more of that Grace, but still only a sufficiency for the moment, because there are no storehouses of Grace. No one can store up enough Grace for tomorrow, anymore than he can store up air in his lungs for tomorrow. Even food stored in storehouses for too long will rot.

Learn the meaning of the word *now:*

> Now "I and my Father are one." [6] Now the
> grace of God is omnipresent to the degree necessary
> at this moment. Let me live in that awareness so that
> Grace feeds, clothes, and houses me at this moment
> and at each succeeding moment. Let me be alert to
> watch for the twelve baskets full left over and
> alert to passing them on.

Unless you are sharing some part of what is given to you, you are making of God's grace something personal directed at you, and then you lose it. What is given to you is not given to you for yourself, but for the world.

Use the Principles To Build a Consciousness

In the metaphysics of the Infinite Way, where you begin to teach the non-power of human thought, human will, human tyranny, and physical might, you can progress only in proportion to your demonstration of this consciousness. Teach the students that at the earliest possible moment they must begin to have periods of practice each day to be aware consciously of the non-power of whatever is claiming power in their household: bad temper, force, indifference, atheism, parasitism, lack of discipline, cleanliness, orderliness, lack of obedience to law. All these things are appearing in the household of beginning students or are at least within range of their experience, and unless they continue to meditate and practice they cannot demonstrate the non-power of the seeming power. As they attain even the tiniest demonstration of non-power, which means the demonstration of the presence of harmony, they have already attained the first experience of Christ-consciousness, and with each practice of this principle they grow in Grace. It is not Grace that grows; it is that they grow in the attainment of the omnipresent Grace which is there in its fullness and always has been there.

All the sins of the world, the false appetites and the diseases, individual and collective, come to your student-body, and you as a teacher have all of the principles with which to build the consciousness that meets these. But for students to hear or read about them is but the first step on the way. Unless you have the power to impart to them the importance of practicing these principles and the further and greater necessity and importance of setting aside those periods of meditation which bring forth the Grace that lifts them higher in consciousness, you are failing as a teacher. No one, by his own effort, can attain Grace. If you could convince students that they should work twelve hours a day, they would not attain Grace. No degree of effort on their part alone will give them Grace. It will only compel them to sit more frequently in those periods of silence to receive the Grace that proves the principles.

Receiving God's grace is not really a religious activity, at least according to what the world looks upon as religion. It is a matter of divine right, divine inheritance, and if a person never heard of a religion or a church he would still be joint-heir to an estate that he will never receive except through meditation.

The Infinite Way is not a religion in the sense of an organized activity devoted to forms of worship, rituals, rites, promises, a concern with what happens after death, or a way of avoiding punishment for sin. It can be thought of as a religion in the sense that it is a revelation of the relationship that exists between God and man and how to attain a realization of that relationship. This is not attained by becoming worthy, by deserving it, or by becoming good. It is attained by the practice of specific metaphysical principles and the meditations that give us the Grace to demonstrate the principles. Knowing all the principles in all the books would not be of much help until a spark of Grace touched a person and made the principles come alive.

For example, you could know that God is infinite power and that disease is not power, and yet you could find yourself without a God and suffering a terrible disease, because knowing these truths intellectually does not give you the grace of God. Knowing that God is infinite and that evil is not power gives you the ability to sit down for a few moments without fear and listen for that "still small voice,"[7] without seeking God, trying to tell God something, or trying to gain His favor. Then in that inner stillness you can receive God's grace, which is indefinable, inexplainable, unknowable. Even after you have experienced It, you will not know what you have experienced, nor can you tell another.

Unceasing Prayer

Be sure that your students are well grounded in the metaphysical principles of the Infinite Way and that they are learning that meditation means, not sitting for an hour without thinking, but having at least a dozen or more periods of from thirty seconds to ten or fifteen minutes in which they open their consciousness to the omnipresence of divine grace, and then get up, knowing that they are endowed from on High. It does not mean that each time students meditate they will receive a message or an impartation from God. It merely means that they have opened themselves, and "in such an hour as ye think not,"[8] sometime during the day when the need arises, the answer will appear in the form necessary.

Gradually as you practice living by unceasing prayer, there will not be a waking moment of your life in which there will not be some area of consciousness listening. As you go to sleep at night, that area of your consciousness will still be receiving and may even wake you up in the middle of the night to give you a message. Do not wait for the periods of meditation to give you messages; meditate, regardless of whether or not there are any messages.

If you, the teacher, have really been faithful in these things, you are doing good healing work, but you are also discovering that you do not know how to heal, and that the truth found in books is not doing the healing work for you. It is merely providing you with the opportunity to reach an inner stillness, a fearlessness, and an unconcern, so that in those moments when God's grace takes over, the appearance is dissolved.

I do not think you will ever know how to heal. I still do not know; I only know that the mail says, "Whereas I was sick, now I am well," or "Whereas I was in pain, now I am free," or "Whereas I was in danger, now I am safe." I know that it is the activity of the Spirit. I have learned that I have no power over any person or over his affairs. I have no power over his false appetite or over his sinful desires or over his sickness. I have no power over the carnal mind. I know only that the release through me of this Grace is a revelation of divine harmony in his experience.

Probably if it should ever be necessary for me or anyone else to learn the how and the why of it, it would be learned, but as of this moment neither I nor any student who has written me, nor any of our teachers, has ever explained what happens. Let me take you a step further. It is not only when you meditate that you may have this awareness of the Spirit which does the healing and protecting work, the reforming, saving, and forgiving work, but rather as you come into the consciousness of unceasing prayer, living continuously with the listening ear, you are living in the divine consciousness of the Spirit. So just as the woman pressed through the throng, touched the hem of the robe and was healed without the Master's knowing she was there, so do people telephone and fail to reach you, write letters and receive healings before the letters are half-way to you, and in many cases, receive healing by merely thinking out toward you.

Does this not prove to you that a human being has no power over a person or over a disease, but that an attained state of consciousness is the light that dispels darkness, without taking thought and without consciously meditating? Let no one believe that he will attain that by saying, "Oh, I do not have to meditate," because it is in the degree of the real meditation, that is, the real stillness in which the "still small voice" operates in you, that you attain and retain that consciousness. In proportion as you learn to live a life of unceasing prayer, an unceasing listening, an abiding in the Word and letting the Word abide in you, do you become the state of Grace that enabled the Master to say, "I am the light of the world."[9] When you have attained that divine state of consciousness, it becomes a state of Grace to your patients, to your students, and ultimately to the world. It is not your personal state of consciousness: it is the divine state of consciousness of which you are individually aware.

Grace To Be the Universal Consciousness

Living by Grace eventually must become the consciousness of mankind universally. I have no inner knowledge as to whether the present troubles of the world are to be resolved peacefully of not. I have no inner knowledge as to whether or not civilization as we know it will be wiped out. I have the knowledge, however, which has been given to me, that future generations are not to be born into the carnal mind, but under Grace, not needing to be taught the Ten Commandments or the Sermon on the Mount, because they will be born into that consciousness and of that consciousness. It will already have been attained, not to be practiced and then attained, but already attained.

Some measure of the spiritual grace which I have attained has enabled the message of the Infinite Way to find outlet through me on a world-wide basis, without any of the human requirements necessary for such an activity. Some of our teachers, practitioners, and students are also attaining things beyond the measure of their human abilities, and they are proving that less and less of the carnal mind is operating.

As I, individually, attain a measure of this Grace-consciousness whereby I live "not by might, nor by power,"[10] but as a beholder of the presence of God going before me to "make the crooked places straight,"[11] preparing "mansions"[12] for me, bringing me the fulfillment of everything necessary to my immediate experience, certain individuals are brought into my experience as students who will gradually become practitioners, and sometimes teachers, proving that they too have attained some measure of that same consciousness of Grace. Then other students are led to the Infinite Way, come under my influence or under the influence of those teachers and practitioners who have attained some measure of Grace, and in the household of those students there is less marital unhappiness, less disease, less juvenile delinquency, less lack and limitation, and on the positive side, more harmony in every department of human life, and a great deal more of love, benevolence, and understanding. The state of Grace attained by one person is in some measure attained by those who come within range of that person's consciousness.

ACROSS THE DESK

The lesson in the letter for this month is a most important one and, because of its importance, deserves serious study and dedicated practice.

As the principles of the Infinite Way are finding ever greater acceptance in the world, students must rise to that higher consciousness to be a light to those still in darkness. Ever more meditation and diligent practice lead to the illumination necessary to lift the consciousness of mankind. It is a glorious work, and we are blessed to be a part of it.

Chapter Eleven

Self-Purification, the Way to the Mystical Consciousness

Throughout the history of the world, there have been some few hundred persons who by the grace of God have received spiritual illumination to a sufficient extent for them to be considered mystics. There also have been a few thousand persons or possibly tens of thousands who by the grace of God have received a touch of the Spirit but, because they did not understand or grasp the meaning or significance of it when it came, could never again regain it or have the experience repeated. These represent one of the saddest elements of society.

It is not necessary for a person to go through life without illumination however, because with an understanding of the truth of being and a consistent living with the principles, the spiritual centers are opened, and it is possible for anyone who earnestly turns to a spiritual teaching to receive a tremendous measure of light. The degree of that illumination varies with the individual and with the use he makes of it after he receives it.

Impersonalization

Illumination is possible only in proportion to our realization of the nature of God as omnipresence and infinity, thereby enabling us to look upon any and every form of discord not as a condition or a person but as a mental imposition, a malpractice, a temptation, a state of hypnotism, a nothingness.

It is virtually impossible to receive spiritual light or illumination and to attain the heights possible through meditation when the mind is divided against itself. If we entertain the belief that God can do something to or for something or somebody, our mind is a house divided against itself. As long as we entertain a belief in two powers, illumination is impossible because that is the barrier that separates us from being that man who has his being in Christ.

We think of each other as having certain qualities, some good and some bad, some spiritual and some material. That is the barrier. We cannot deny that some of us are more materially-minded, more sensually-minded, or more money-minded than others. But that is not true of the person in his spiritual identity: it is true only of whatever of impersonal human qualities he is manifesting.

It would be foolish not to recognize that a wrong is being done and that we are witnessing a form of error if we should see a man in the act of stealing a wallet. But as long as we call that man a thief we cannot open our consciousness to spiritual illumination because we cannot entertain truth while our mind is filled with error. A truth and a lie cannot fill the same space at the same time. If we do behold a man in the act of stealing a wallet, however, let us be sure that we remember quickly, "This is the carnal mind in action." Thereby we have impersonalized the error; we have taken it away from the person and placed it out in space, and the moment we have done that with real conviction, it dissolves. It now has no avenue of expression; it has no person through whom to operate.

Nothingizing

After impersonalizing, the next step is to nothingize the carnal mind, that is, to realize that a carnal mind cannot be constituted of God-qualities because if it were it would be eternal and immortal and as good as God. Therefore, if it is not created by God, it was not created and so it can exist only as a state of illusion, a state of belief, or a state of hypnotism. Through this work we keep our mind pure, full of truth, and thus open to spiritual illumination which cannot happen while we are holding a person in condemnation.

This is the whole basis of our healing work. Unless we are able to hold no one in judgment, we cannot bring about spiritual peace. Disease of every name and nature is handled this way, and so is every form of sin or false appetite, marital relations, employer and employee relations, unemployment, and capital and labor relations.

Humanly in one way or another, we might bring peace between capital and labor or between employer and employee, but we could not bring spiritual harmony into that scene because in our mind we would be accepting one side as right and one as wrong. In the whole of the spiritual kingdom, however, there is neither a right side nor a wrong side: there is only a spiritual side which is eternal harmony.

As Infinite Way students, we have no right to go into a prison to do work of any nature at all, unless we have reached the understanding that we are not trying to reform or regenerate anybody, and neither are we going in to teach anybody. We recognize that which appears to need regeneration as the carnal mind.

Lifting the Burden

The world that believes there are good and evil men and women, that believes that there is a man or a woman who has sinned, is sinning, or will sin is this world that sits in judgment. Not so the Christ! The Christ says, "Judge not according to the appearance, but judge righteous judgment.[1]. . .Why callest thou me good? there is none good but one, that is, God.[2]. . . Neither do I condemn thee."[3] We are not the Christ-mind while we have a right and a wrong, a good and a bad, a sick and a well.

The only way that we can come to that state of consciousness is by understanding, first, that God constitutes individual being and has manifested Itself as individual being. Every individual in the world is God in expression, the one mind and the one life, the one soul, and the one spirit individually manifest. God appearing as individual being is a universal spiritual truth and has nothing to do with appearances. Since "God is no respecter of persons,"[4] this is the truth about us and also about everyone in jail and everyone in a hospital.

The healing Christ is the state of consciousness that knows that truth and then knows that no man is evil and no man is good. All good manifested by man is God in expression; all evil is the acceptance of two powers, good and evil, sick and well, sinful and pure. The Christ-mind separates evil from the individual and places it where it belongs in the carnal mind that is tempting us to accept two powers. Having placed it there, we have taken the burden from our shoulders and we no longer have a guilt complex.

If there is one person anywhere who can look through the appearance and understand that anything we have done or are doing of an erroneous nature is not we, but merely our ignorance of the fact that we are being tempted by an impersonal source and in our ignorance acting out from that temptation, he can lift the burden.

We cannot condemn a person for making a mistake, nor can we condemn a person for doing something in ignorance. All sin and all disease are the product of the ignorance of the great truth that God constitutes individual being and that any and every phase of discord is the carnal mind. Thus we lift the burden from the person: from the man in prison, in the hospital, in the saloon, or in the gambling house. We lift it from him and we place it out here where it has no law, no activity, no cause, no person. Now it is dead, and we can rest in that truth.

The Christ-State of Consciousness Is Sought Out by Others

If we were in our office or home and our telephone bell were ringing every minute and a half with another person calling for help, our entire treatment would take place between one call and the next. No matter what was said to us, we would keep that up all day and all night because we would not connect it with a person but with the impersonal carnal mind and we would be nothingizing it even while they were talking. When we hang up the receiver, we can rest in the truth, rest until the telephone rings again about thirty seconds later.

We can be assured that as we become clear on these points that is exactly what will happen. It happens to all persons who come to the Christ-state of consciousness. They draw unto themselves all those who want to be released from condemnation, ignorance, sin, fear, darkness. All those who are struggling are drawn to the light. The person who has attained Christ-consciousness does not have to advertise. He does not have to let it be known what he knows or what he teaches; he does not have to wear a robe. He will be hunted out; he will be chased up every alley until he sheds the light and shares it.

All the Christ-mind is, is the mind of a person who does not accept or believe in two powers, who does not sit in judgment or condemnation on any person or thing. The evil political or commercial leaders, the evil self-seeking industrial tycoons or labor union leaders will exist in the human scene until we understand that it is impossible for man to be evil, selfish, or unjust. All there is to man is God made manifest because God constitutes individual being. This is the truth about everything on the face of the globe: human, animal, vegetable, or mineral. All is God in individual expression.

Psychology Does Not Enter into the Healing Practice

With every appearance we must, first of all, impersonalize it.

We do not tell anyone that he can be helped if he reads ten pages of a book, goes to church, tithes, is grateful, or loving. This may be effective on the psychological level, that is, if a human being could change his nature. Years ago a comedian, who claimed to have a sure cure for alcoholism, said that all a person has to do when he lifts a glass of liquor to his mouth is to open his hand. Of course, we all know that that is a sure cure. But how does an alcoholic come to the place where he can open that hand?

So many times a person is told, "If only you could be more loving! If you could just be more forgiving! If you were more generous, more grateful! Ah, you have missed three Sundays in church! If you would read so many pages!" That is all nonsense because it is doubtful that psychologically a person can change his nature. Only the activity of the Christ in his consciousness can do that. When a person tries to change humanly through willpower or repression, he is likely to explode some day. To become different from what we are, it is necessary that the Christ be introduced into our consciousness.

One way of doing that is to find the person who is willing, not only willing but able, to guide us through whatever experience it is—sin, disease, lack or death—without criticism or judgment, without condemnation, without trying to improve us, without moralizing or preaching, an individual who is able to hold steadfast in the realization, "This has nothing to do with you. It is an activity of the carnal mind, that belief in good and evil, a hypnotic suggestion. It is just nothing but a mental imposition. It has nothing to do with a person. In the final analysis, it is the fleshly mind, a nothingness and does not have to be fought or overcome, just recognized for its nothingness." And then that person rests in that word.

This is how Infinite Way healing work is accomplished. It has nothing to do with prayers that try to influence God; it has nothing to do with finding somebody so holy that God is going to do something through him that God will not do through someone else. It has to do with specific principles.

The Ability To Impersonalize Makes a Person a Transparency for God

When we fully grasp the idea that all evil is impersonal, that very moment our consciousness is ready to be a transparency through which God appears, a transparency through which the Christ is made manifest. But our consciousness cannot be a transparency while it is double-minded, while it has good and evil in it. None of us can be wholly pure, but we become a transparency for the Christ in proportion to our ability to impersonalize all evil.

How often do we accept whatever temptation is in the air! Somebody says there is an epidemic, and we get sick! We accept the mental imposition which we have the power to reject. The world cannot do this because it does not know the truth of impersonalization, and therefore has no defense against sin, disease, lack, or limitation. But this is the principle with which we work, and this is the reason our meditations are successful.

If we are not successful, we can be sure that we are double-minded and are sitting in judgment, criticism, or condemnation. We have not fulfilled the teaching of Jesus Christ which says: "Therefore if thou bring thy gift to the altar, and there rememberest that thy brother hath ought against thee: Leave there thy gift before the altar, and go thy way; first be reconciled to thy brother, and then come and offer thy gift."[5]

Purification Is a Continuous Process

As long as we have not purified ourselves, we cannot be at peace. Let us not forget that we cannot purify ourselves once and stay that way any more than we can take a bath once and stay clean. Purification is a continuous process, not for a year or two, but forever as far as I am concerned. It is praying without ceasing. The world mesmerism is so strong that it will reach through into our consciousness unless we are alert and are able quickly and constantly to impersonalize. Once we can do that, our mind is not warring with anybody or anything, and then we can meditate.

The mind will be still if there is no inner warfare going on. But there is always warfare if we believe in two powers: in good and evil. If we have desires, if we are still struggling to attain or achieve something, the mind cannot be at rest. There is no reason really to be struggling for anything, especially anything of a spiritual nature, because the very struggle itself will prevent our attaining it. The struggle is mental, and as long as there is a mental activity, we do not have the Spirit. It is only when we realize, "I already am," that the struggle is over. The struggle is all gone if we realize this mystical truth which is universal and has been revealed by every mystic.

The Essence of Mysticism Is I Am

One of the accounts of the search for God that has always interested me is that of a young Moslem woman, a mystic who joined a pilgrimage to Mecca. The Moslems are taught that if they can get to Mecca, if only once in their lifetime, they will be saved forever. Everything is wiped out, and their whole life will then be lived with God. So every year from every part of the Moslem world, there are pilgrimages to Mecca. This young woman who had joined such a pilgrimage had a difficult time of it, crossing mountains and streams, through hot weather, stormy weather, and cold weather, and experienced all the inconveniences of travel that existed a couple of hundred years ago.

Eventually they came to the outskirts of Mecca. Everyone then broke into a run to rush right into Mecca. But something halted this girl. She stopped, began to think, and finally dropped to her knees. "God forgive me for coming all this way to find You in Mecca, You who had found me where I was." She saw that there was no need to travel.

The Master centuries ago said, "The hour cometh, when ye

shall neither in this mountain, nor yet at Jerusalem, worship the Father.[6] . . . The kingdom of God cometh not with observation: Neither shall they say, Lo here! or, Lo there! for, behold, the kingdom of God is within you."[7]

That realization brings us to the great mystical truth, I Am, which Moses gave to the world. "I Am That I Am."[8] After that he was no longer a shepherd: he was a leader of men, a spiritual leader because of his realization of I Am. Jesus, too, realized the *I Am*. He said, "I am the bread of life.[9] . . . I am the resurrection, and the life"[10] not, "I am searching; I am seeking; I am hoping; I am praying," but "Now I have come to the realization *I Am.*"

The realization of *I Am* made a shepherd a great leader. That recognition of *I Am* made a Hebrew rabbi the light of the Christian world. It makes no difference what we are or where we are when the realization of *I Am* comes to us. From that moment on we are not that person at all: we are the light of our particular world.

Furthermore, it really makes no difference where we turn in the mystical writings: Persian, Moslem, Hindu, Chinese, or Japanese mystics, or the Christian mystics of the twelfth to the seventeenth centuries. They have all given the same message: *I Am*. That is the essence of mysticism, and when that realization is attained it gives us freedom. Why? Because in that *I Am*-ness there is no longer a desire for anything or anybody; there is no longer an ambition, there is no longer any strife or any struggle: there is a resting in that realization. Then everything necessary for our fulfillment—whether it is a person, a place, a thing, a circumstance, or a condition—automatically flows into existence.

It is easier to rise to the mystical experience after we have made a specific practice of impersonalizing and nothingizing because when we are not fighting powers apart from God, we are resting in *I Am*-ness. "The Lord is my shepherd."[11] If the Lord is our shepherd we shall not want, and there is nothing left to fight for. We can rest in confidence and assurance. As long as there is opposition in our mind, as long as there is judgment, as long as there is duality—two powers—there is no way of our realizing *I Am*. It is only when we have learned to impersonalize and nothingize that our consciousness is so clear and so transparent that the spiritual light of the Christ shines through. It is this Presence that goes before us to make the way straight.

A Yielding of Material Sense Is Necessary

Regardless of how true and pure our vision is, however, we cannot remove the effect of something without removing the cause of it, and if an individual is rigidly maintaining within himself erroneous traits, the condition of health or supply will not change until the state of consciousness has changed. When the state of consciousness changes, its externalization has to change because the cause is no longer there.

And what is the cause? It is our ignorance which makes us accept two powers and makes us personalize. Most of us are not tenacious in our hates, envies, jealousies, or mad ambitions, regardless of the fact that we all have some of these traits, and always have had. But they are not what might be called deep or strong, and so when we come into contact with a consciousness that is not holding us in condemnation, our consciousness changes very easily.

When, however, a practitioner hits up against those who are adamant in their evil habits, want to cling to them, and have no desire to be free of them, then it is more difficult to bring the light to that consciousness. Many times the practitioner will have to stand fast with a patient, sometimes for a long time, until there is a yielding within the patient.

Spiritual healing is not merely adding health to an erroneous state of consciousness. Spiritual healing is bringing us to the position of yielding up material sense, twoness, duality. As students take up a study of this nature, they very often find conditions in their body changing and improving, and wonder why one thing or another thing persists while other things have cleared up. There is only one answer: they have not yet come to the complete surrender where they are willing to grant that God constitutes their being and that they are wholly pure. When they come to that point, they find that discords rarely abide in them.

The Clear Setting Forth of Principles Makes Self-Purification Easier

In the beginning, purification of our selfhood does not have anything to do with trying to become better human beings. That is only the effect of the purification. The purification itself means the ability to have that mind which was in Christ Jesus, meaning the mind that does not judge, criticize, or condemn, that does not accept two powers, and that can impersonalize and nothingize. That is all there is to self-purification, but the act of self-purification by this means results outwardly in a changed state of what appears as human consciousness. Erroneous human traits begin to dissolve and ultimately disappear, probably not leaving us perfect in this world, but working in that direction. Now since the principles have been set forth so specifically in Infinite Way tape recordings and writings, it is going to be easier for every serious student of the Infinite Way to attain this purified spiritual state of consciousness that realizes God is individual being, and therefore impersonalize every appearance of evil.

The letter of truth is found in all Infinite Way writings, but it has not been understood by our students, nor has it been practiced by them even if or when they have understood it. They have given more attention to the mystical, inspirational side than, first of all, learning and practicing these specific principles until consciousness is developed.

If Infinite Way students are to attain the mystical consciousness, it will come about through the study and practice of the principles which lead to a purification of consciousness, because there can be no degree of mystical or spiritual consciousness as long as there is an acceptance of good and evil—two powers—of the personalization of good and evil, or of consciously or unconsciously battling evil, trying to overcome it in an attempt to heal disease, sin, fear, or lack.

Your Consciousness and Christ-Consciousness

As our consciousness accepts the truth that we need not fight because the battle is not ours, as we are able to be that consciousness which does not take up the sword and engage in physical or mental battles, we are developing this Christ-consciousness that does not resist evil but abides in the word: "Thou, Pilate, hast no power over me, for there is only one power and that is of God."

With that conviction our progress will be more rapid. It will show itself forth in doing better and quicker healing work. And it must show itself forth in our attainment of a greater degree of Christ-consciousness because the more these particular principles are practiced, the more Christ-consciousness is developing in us, and the more of a transparency we are for the activity of the Christ. This is the mystical consciousness.

Christ-consciousness is our consciousness when we acknowledge no evil to combat, when evil has been impersonalized and nothingized. Christ-consciousness is not some consciousness that is going to come to us. It is our present consciousness when our consciousness is divested of personalizing good and evil or giving power to evil. This very consciousness which is you is Christ-consciousness in proportion as you are impersonalizing and nothingizing.

There is no new consciousness to gain, no other consciousness to seek; it is a purification of the consciousness which we now have which, in its purified state, is Christ-consciousness. In other words, after his illumination, Moses was still Moses, but with a purified consciousness. Jesus was still Jesus, but with that purified or Christ-consciousness. That is why he is called Jesus the Christ, Jesus the enlightened. He is still the same Jesus, but now not unenlightened.

Enlightenment means only one thing: the recognition of these principles, regardless of how they are stated. That is what constitutes enlightenment and opens the way for illumination. The inner experiences that come to us, as well as the instruction, the wisdom, the guidance, and the direction come only at those times when we are living in the consciousness of no condemnation, of impersonalization, and they cannot come to us at any other time. That is the full meaning of the statement that when we go to the altar to pray and there remember that anyone has ought against us we must first get up and make peace. Until we have come to the realization that God constitutes his being and that the condition is the impersonal carnal mind, we have no ability to heal, and our prayers will not reach any further than our own mind.

The Enlightened Consciousness Is the Healing Consciousness

What we really do when we undertake healing for someone is to lift the person above the physical plane of consciousness where the laws of physicality are not operating. Then spiritual harmony takes hold of him. When we engage in spiritual healing work, we are not healing the body of a person; we are not doing anything to the organs or functions of a body. All we are doing is lifting the person in consciousness above the physical and the mental plane to where he is under the grace of God, which wipes out the physical and the mental laws that have been binding him. That is how spiritual healing is accomplished.

Spiritual consciousness nullifies mental laws, the mental law of malpractice, the laws of belief, the laws of mesmeric suggestion, and in lifting the patient above the mind, these mental laws are nullified. So, too, there are physical laws—laws of germs, infection, contagion, climate—but when the patient is lifted into the higher dimension of consciousness those laws do not operate.

Even though infections and contagions may rage all around us, although there may be panics, depressions, unemployment, and limitations of every form, they do not come nigh our dwelling place. Why? Because we are not dwelling there: we are dwelling "in the secret place of the most High"[12]; we are dwelling in the mystical consciousness of our oneness with the Father where life is lived by Grace, not by physical laws and not by mental laws.

Every spiritual demonstration is an annulling or a wiping out of the operation of a physical or a mental law. It is lifting us into a realm of consciousness where the particular physical or mental law from which we are suffering no longer operates.

Living mentally and physically means determining what we want and how we are going to get it. Living spiritually is yielding ourselves to the reign of God. It is a yielding of desires, a yielding of the self to a receptivity to spiritual guidance. It is not an outlining and a determining of what we want or how we are going to attain it: it is a complete yielding of one's self so that one may be the instrument through which divine intelligence can operate.

ACROSS THE DESK

Every four years as attention in the United States is focused upon the selection of the President and Vice President of the United States, Infinite Way students are reminded of how important it is to realize that "the government is on His shoulders." The "ten" righteous men, those who know this truth, can play a significant role in bringing to pass God's government "on earth as it is in heaven."

An election is an opportunity for citizens to exercise the franchise and vote for the candidates of their choice. In order to vote intelligently and fulfill his responsibility as a citizen, every voter should be thoroughly familiar with the issues and know how each candidate stands on these issues, not only in terms of what he says, but in terms of his record. This is the responsibility of an informed citizenry, and Infinite Way students should fall into that category.

Over and above that, and even more important, is the meditation or spiritual work in which each student engages to the end that citizens are not swayed by the carnal mind and the highly charged emotional promotional activities characteristic of a typical Presidential campaign. Each student should realize that the universal human mind, with its lust for power, greed, and self-seeking, is not power in the realized presence of God; that this election as an activity for the preservation of freedom, is taking place within the one Consciousness which is intelligence and love; and that only *I* votes. That *I* is the divine Consciousness individualized. It is guided by a wisdom beyond human understanding and is, therefore, unerring in its judgment.

For further enlightenment on this all-important area of government, study the following material in Joel's writings:

Living Now, pp. 175-178.
Altitude of Prayer, pp. 127-129.
Realization of Oneness, chap. 12.
Our Spiritual Resources, chap. 10.
The Contemplative Life, chap. 7.
The 1959 Infinite Way Letters, pp. 137-144.
Beyond Words and Thoughts, pp. 190-193; chap 7.
Consciousness Is What I Am, pp. 53-55

Finally, I quote from *Our Spiritual Resources,* a call to all students to be alert, written by Joel, just before the 1960 Presidential election:

Our Privilege and Duty

"Right now, nothing is more important for Infinite Way students than daily prayer on the subject of international relations.

"Our students can be neither Republicans, Democrats, Socialists, nor Communists. We are functioning spiritually, and our realization is that *all* government is on His shoulders—never at the mercy of man. Our daily realization is that the carnal mind is impersonal and has no person through whom to act as an instrument or means of action. God constitutes the government on earth as in heaven, and the belief in two powers is nullified as we understand its operation to be devoid of spiritual life or law."

TAPE RECORDED EXCERPTS
Prepared by the Editor

Voting Wisely

"Let no one find in your consciousness condemnation. This doesn't mean that you don't have opinions. You are perhaps more firmly established in your opinion if you have spiritual wisdom than would otherwise be the case. This doesn't mean being foolish and saying, 'What difference does it make who governs our country or what kind of a parliament or congress we have?' or 'Let anybody get in there because they're all spiritual.' That's really stupidity. . . . If we have the consciousness of man's true identity, it will be pointed out to us who comes nearest to approaching that. . . . Thus we are guided to vote for the right candidate, the right party at any given time."

Joel S. Goldsmith, "Grace," *The 1958 London Advanced Class.*

Chapter Twelve

The Ye-Shall-Know-the-Truth Way

The spiritual or contemplative life is a specific way of life that has a specific purpose. It is one on which a person does not embark unthinkingly or without a reason, nor is it something that one arbitrarily chooses. Furthermore, there is a specific method of introducing this way of life into consciousness and of applying it to daily life.

Normally, human beings have very little control over their lives or their destiny. They are subject, for example, to weather and climate, to the limitations of their education, and they are usually subject to the mores of their particular world. So many circumstances outside and beyond their control govern their lives that it is almost ludicrous to say that any human being is master of his own fate.

But it has been known throughout all time, and it is now being introduced again into the world, that this need not be so, although in this age, it is easy to be tempted by current psychological beliefs into believing that we are victims of circumstances beyond our control. It is not necessary, however, for a person to fall afoul of all the evils that beset humankind, because every individual, free or slave, has within himself the God-given capacity to rise above and out of his condition in life. Slave races from all parts of the globe have broken out of their slavery; downtrodden people of all races have attained emancipation, freedom, and sometimes great glory.

Your Good Is Not Dependent on Time or Circumstances

No one is born without an inner capacity for God-living and God-expression, but the one thing necessary is to know the truth. Because a thousand may fall at your left and ten thousand at your right, it does not follow that these evils need come near your dwelling place. It does follow, however, that you are the only one who can prevent them from touching you or your affairs. This is not something that anyone can do for you, not your parents, your family, or your children: it is something that you, alone, can and must do. The responsibility rests with every individual, first, to learn what the truth is, and then to begin to live in contemplation of that truth, knowing it, until eventually the particular experience which sets him free takes place.

Your life is not the beneficiary or the victim of what your parents have done or have not done, nor what your children or your neighbors do or do not do. It is what *you* do, and if *you* dwell "in the secret place of the most High,"[1] you will find safety and security, peace and joy.

The Master, Christ Jesus, gave the formula in the parable of the vine and the branches when he said that if you do not abide in the Word and let the Word abide in you, you will be as a branch of a tree that is cut off and withers. Always the emphasis is on *you.* It has nothing to do with what your community does; it has nothing to do with what the times or conditions of the world may be. Always it has to do with *you.* Always the Master spoke to the individual—to *you.* If *you* abide in the Word, certain effects will follow, but if *you* do not abide in the Word, the results will not be what you would like. So the responsibility is always on *you.*

Jesus was a great individualist. He realized that life is strictly an individual matter. Each one of us comes into this world alone; each one goes out alone. Each one of us alone is responsible for every step of the way, and that is why sometimes in the same families there is success, and sometimes failure or mediocrity.

What *you* do determines your experience, not whether you are a member of a prominent family or an obscure one. Sometimes, being a member of an illustrious family may prove to be disastrous, even when it would seem that it should be beneficial.

God, the Rock

There is but one God, and that God is within you. He is with you if you mount up to heaven; He is with you if you make your bed in hell; He is with you if you "walk through the valley of the shadow of death."[2] God will function in your experience in the moment of your recognition of Him. Whatever your state of being is—purity or sin, wealth or poverty, health or disease— there is still only one Father, one God, and that One, indivisible, infinite, omnipresent, omnipotent, omniscient, a God that cannot be influenced.

All the prayers that were ever prayed will not move God one iota. Not all the prayers that have been written, printed, or voiced will ever move God. Try it some time. Even if, just as an experiment, you could get the whole world to pray all at one time to have God set the sun back one hour or bring it up one hour sooner, or if you went to church and prayed to God to have peace on earth tomorrow, you would soon find out how impossible it is to move God, to influence, or to affect Him in any way. You cannot stop God from being God. You cannot stop God from being God by being in or out of a religion, not by your sins or by your purity. God is, and no one is ever going to change that.

Your Sowing
Determines Your Reaping

One of these days, as you follow the contemplative way of life, you will know why it is inevitable that every sin brings forth punishment, whether it is a sin of omission or commission. Punishment has nothing to do with God: it has to do with the law of cause and effect, the karmic law. You set in motion that which comes back to you. You do it—not God! You do it!

All you have to be concerned about is that you are not setting in motion today some thought or thing that is going to react upon you tomorrow. Only what you consciously know can take place in your experience. What you know you demonstrate, and what you make a part of your consciousness is what you bring forth into expression.

Does this mean, then, that you are responsible for all the evils and ills experienced or being experienced in your life? In one sense, yes. You are responsible in this way: through ignorance. Through ignorance of the one God, you have become an antenna for the world's beliefs, so that if the world believes that you must catch cold because of inclement weather today, four, five, or six out of ten will catch cold. As each universal belief flits through the air, because of ignorance, a person becomes a victim of whatever the universal belief may be.

"Choose you this day whom ye will serve."[3] Each day, you are called upon to make a choice as to whether your life is to be governed by current beliefs circulating in the world or by the activity of the infinite, invisible Spirit, omnipresent and omnipotent.

When the spirit of God dwells in you, you become the instrument of God. You then have no capacity *of your own:* you have no capacity to do or to be; you lose the capacity to be sick or well, good or bad. You have only the capacity to show forth God's glory, and you are then an externalization of the Infinite Invisible that is governing you.

Spiritual Fruitage

The fruitage of the contemplative way of life is attained by daily making a decision, when you awaken in the morning and even before you are out of bed, to set the scene for the entire day:

> This day is a messenger of God; this day brings
> into my experience God's grace, God's law, God's life,
> God's presence, and God's power.
>
> This day, I choose whom I will serve.
> My heart, my soul, and my mind are filled with the
> conscious realization of the presence of God.
> I surrender myself unto God. I listen for the still
> small voice, that It may guide, lead, and direct me.

That is how you begin to put into practice the ye-shall-know-the-truth way. You are choosing now, and thereby you are sowing to the Spirit. Throughout the day, you will take two, three, or five minutes for brief reminders:

> This day is bringing the presence and power of
> God into my experience. This day is revealing God's
> glory. "The heavens declare the glory of God; and the
> firmament showeth his handiwork.[4]. . . This is the
> day which the Lord hath made; I will rejoice and be
> glad in it."[5] Every moment of every day, God's grace
> is being revealed in my experience.

Living As a Beholder

As you progress in your practice of the contemplative way of life, the form of your contemplation takes on a different character, and you become a beholder of God in action. It is much

the same as your attitude might be when you are up early
enough in the morning to see a sunrise and then at evening a
sunset, and you realize that you have had no part in bringing
these about. You cannot make these things happen. Again as
you watch the flowers growing in the garden and the trees sway-
ing in the wind, you are merely beholding God's grace in action.
Awaken, then, in the morning and look over your shoulder,
almost as if you had stepped an inch in back of yourself:

> Throughout this day, I will be a beholder of God
> at work. I will not try to influence God;
> I will not try to get God to do something for me:
> I will merely behold what God is doing.

Whatever your work may be, you can always step an inch in
back of yourself and behold what things God is bringing into
expression for you, this minute, an hour from now, two hours,
five hours—always watching what God is doing, not only in
your experience, but in that of the world.

The contemplative life leads you from one experience to
another, until the final stage is reached in which the beholder
and that which is beheld become one, just as the branch of a tree
is not separate and apart from the tree itself. There is no longer
God *and* you; there is no longer a *you;* there is only God, a
Presence that is always with you as your protection, safety, security, peace, and harmony.

Through the practice of the contemplative way of life, the
branch is grafted back on to the trunk of the tree so that the
branch no longer has a life of its own. In fact, the branch is not
a branch any more. It is part of the tree, and when you look at
it, you no longer say, "Oh, you're a branch," but you look at the
tree and say, "You are a tree." That is the final revelation, that
revelation in which you realize that you are the Life; you are the
very Life that animates your being, the very Life, the very
Wisdom, the very Intelligence, the very Love.

One Father: All Heirs

Once you are consciously one—and do not forget that word *consciously*—once you are consciously one with God, you are no longer living your own life: your life is being lived for you, in you, through you, and as you by the Life Itself. The Life is your life: infinite, immortal, and eternal life. That invisible Life which is at work in the ground, in the branch, and in the trunk is operating upon one seed, making it a tree, and upon another kind of seed, bringing forth a human life. When you understand that that Life is your life, that that Invisible is the very being of you, the presence, the power, the wisdom, the intelligence, and the love, then you are consciously one with It, and It can fulfill Itself in your experience.

Think what would happen to your relationship with another if each one could accept the truth that there is but one Father, could accept Jesus' teaching, "Call no man your father upon the earth."[6] Think what would happen if you acknowledged that you and all mankind are brothers and sisters. Jealousy would go out the window along with envy, malice, lust, greed, and fear. If you and I are brothers and sisters, what have we to fear?

In a real family relationship, there is only one pocketbook, and everyone in that family is entitled to a share of it. The father earns it, and all the members of the family are entitled to dip into it. In the spiritual family, God is the Father, and everyone is an heir, so that no one has need of anything from another; and therefore he does not try to get anything from another. He has no need of stealing or lying, because there is one Father, and every person is joint-heir to His riches.

Think! Think, if only a handful of people could fully accept the truth that there is only one Father and accept that Father as the universal source of their supply, of their life, their love, their protection, they would never again look to one another, except to share, as families do—brothers and sisters of one household. Think how they share! Then think what the effect on the world would be as it witnessed a group here or a group there, actually living in love because of the recognition that there is but one Father, one Source.

As you meditate in contemplation of such truth as this and find yourself at-one with your source, you receive inspiration that manifests itself in your business, art, or profession, ideas that you could never have dreamed of—powers and strength of which you yourself are not capable. You find yourself the outlet for an infinite source. That really is the ultimate object of the contemplative way of life—not living as a separate branch running up and down the world, but as a branch of a tree that is part of the whole, drawing its all from the center of its own being through an invisible, infinite activity of Good.

There could be just as many religions on earth as there are today and just as many churches, and yet every person could live in peace on earth and good will to men, once the acknowledgment is made that there is only one Father and that all of this is not to be found in the books of the church or the music of the church or its ceremonies or rites, but in you— *in you*—wherever you may be or whatever your present condition may be. Then you can worship inside or outside a church, and better than that, you can even worship in one another's churches.

Good As Unfolding Grace

The contemplative life is a continuous recognition that whatever healing, regeneration, or good takes place in your experience is for God's glory, the glory of God revealing Itself as the branch that you are.

By your continuous contemplation of this truth of the source of life and your contact with It, as a branch of the Tree of Life, all that the Tree is, you become. Its life becomes your life; Its wisdom, your wisdom; Its protection, your protection; and in all this, you are not going out looking to anybody for anything, not asking for his cooperation or his understanding, not asking for his gifts. You abide in the center of your being, realizing that because of your oneness with the Tree of Life, which is God, you are the showing forth of all that God is. Then you are in the position that the Master was, able to heal and feed the multitudes, not by virtue of yourself, but by virtue of your conscious recognition of your oneness with the source.

In your oneness with God, all good is yours by the grace of God, without taking it from anyone else and, furthermore, because of its spiritual nature, it is multiplied in the life of every individual who bears witness to this truth.

The contemplative way of life holds tremendous satisfactions, even though at first it may appear to have certain limitations. For example, it deprives a person of the great pleasure he sometimes feels in being able to blame others for his failure, unhappiness, or misery. Scapegoating can no longer be indulged in because he has now learned that whatever he has blundered into of an erroneous nature in life has been because of his own ignorance of spiritual principles, and at any moment in his life he can begin to lead the contemplative life by his recognition of his oneness with the source, and then patiently watch how the outer picture gradually begins to conform to this inner grace.

The Normalcy of the Contemplative Life

Those who undertake the contemplative way of life live normal lives outwardly. They remain in the same business, art, or profession, right where they are, but eventually something takes place within them that begins to change the outer circumstances of their life and sometimes puts them into a different work, a different profession, or brings out talents of an artistic nature that they never knew were dormant within them.

An individual begins the contemplative way of life where he is, and the outside world—not even the members of his family—need ever know that he is living it, because it is taking place within his own consciousness, and he need never speak of that unless he has a desire to do so. I can assure you that with all my traveling around the world, I never speak of this to any person I meet, except in the course of my public work where people are led to me for that purpose. Never do I speak of it to persons I meet on the plane or in the hotel. It is my individual demonstration, and if someone is led to me, I share it with him, but not unless he requests it.

So it is, then, that this life of inner contemplation should begin without any outward change in your mode of living. The entire change is within you, because much of the time that you might waste in idle dreaming, in listening to the radio, watching television, or lying in bed before you go to sleep or before it is time to get up will be spent in inner contemplation. There is always time for contemplation for the person who really wants to live the contemplative life.

From Thinking Thoughts
to Receiving Inner Assurance

By continuous practice of meditation you are led to a certain experience which comes to you in meditation. That is the point where you are not thinking thoughts of any nature, but a thought comes and wells up from within you—a thought that you did not consciously put in motion.

Remember, up to this time during your contemplation, you have consciously thought thoughts; you have consciously put into action this contemplative thinking. Ultimately, a time comes when you are really not thinking at all, when a thought pops into you and sometimes it is so audible that you look around and wonder who said it and are surprised to find that there was nobody there to say it. Then you realize that it must have come to you from within.

At other times, it is not audible, but you know that it happened, that you heard or sensed it because you received an impartation, a message, guidance, or something from within.

That is when you begin the second phase of the spiritual life, that is, the period of meditation. In this period of meditation, you do not do the thinking: you do the hearing. You receive the assurance from within, impartations, guidance, direction, and if nothing else, just the feeling that God is on the field. When you have the assurance of God, you need nothing else, because God is taking care of all the details.

When you are governed by God and are leading the spiritual life, you do not have to be told what God is going to do for you tomorrow; in fact, you do not have to be told anything beyond the truth, "I will never leave thee, nor forsake thee."[7] With that assurance, you can undertake anything and everything. You need nothing more.

You do not have to ask where the capital you may need is to come from; you do not have to ask where the ideas are going to come from. You just go about your business once this assurance has been given you. It is like a little child crossing the street with his mother. A child needs no greater assurance than to feel his mother's hand in his. His mother does not have to say, "We are going to cross the street, and I am going to guide you through the automobiles and protect you from being hurt." No, a long as the child feels his mother's hand, he has no fear.

So it is in the spiritual way of life. From the moment you feel that the presence of God is with you, from the moment It has announced Itself to you, you need take no thought for your life. You need take no thought for what tomorrow will bring because your hand is in God's hand, and you can trust all the rest of your days and nights, your business and everything else into that keeping. It will lead and steer you, guide and protect you, clothe, house, and feed you.

The Goal

The object of the spiritual way of life is not attaining health, supply, companionship, or success. The goal of this life is to attain the conscious awareness of the presence of God—the conscious realization of a Presence—of *the* Presence, a conscious realization that *I* am with you. From that moment on, your whole life is lived in an inner communion with the Father who has now revealed Himself to you.

Be assured that the Father is within you because the kingdom of God is within you. The only reason you are not in constant communion with the Father is because your human life has brought about a separation.

Too young, you were told that God is up there, out there, or far off. You were taught to fear Him or taught that God is going to punish you if you look to the left or to the right. In other words, you never entered into a relationship with God as Father as Jesus did or a relationship with God as Friend as Abraham did; and for that reason you have lost your contact with this Presence that is within you.

Through contemplation and through the recognition of the truth that God is not a punishing or a rewarding God, but just a Presence—the all-life, the all-being—you begin to tabernacle with God and to commune inwardly with Him. This leaves you in a constant state of realization of an invisible Presence, and then you can say with Paul, "I live; yet not I, but Christ liveth in me.[8]. . . I can do all things through Christ which strengtheneth me."[9]

The contemplative or spiritual way of life leads to the experience of the unveiling of the Christ. It leads to a point in meditation in which you come face to face with God and receive a direct inner assurance:

> Walk in the way I have shown you. I will
> never leave you, nor forsake you. I will be with you,
> even to the end of the world. Fear not! Fear not!
> Nothing from without can enter to disturb or harm
> you. Fear not all the strength of the enemy. Fear not!
> Fear not, for I am with you.

Then there is no use asking what God is going to do, how He is going to do it, or when. Then there is no longer any roving around of the human mind. There is just a resting, a resting always in the assurance: "I in the midst of you am mighty."

ACROSS THE DESK

For unto us a child is born,
unto us a son is given: and the government shall be
upon his shoulder: and his name shall be called
Wonderful, Counsellor, the mighty God,
the everlasting Father, The Prince of Peace.

Of the increase of his government and
peace there shall be no end.

Isaiah 9:6,7

To each of us comes that glorious day when the Child is born in us, that is, when we awaken to that son of God in the midst of us, which has been waiting for our recognition. Unbeknownst to us, It has been with us in our joys and sorrow, our triumphs and defeats, our successes and failures, patiently waiting for our acknowledgment of Its presence, persistently knocking at the door of our consciousness. But in our spiritual dullness we have not been aware of its gentle nudging.

Then the moment of awakening comes when we know It is with us and will be with us always. That moment is our Christmas, and for us the world is wrapped in the eternal stillness and silence of our consciousness of peace into which the noises of the outer world can no longer penetrate. May that Christ-peace be yours this holy season and the real Christmas be celebrated in your heart.

TAPE RECORDED EXCERPTS
Prepared by the Editor

Since unfoldment is infinite, we can always go deeper and attain greater awareness. Why not begin that deepening process by working with one principle until it becomes realized consciousness? The outline below emphasizes the all-important principle of the nature of spiritual power, pointing up ways of making it your very own.

"One Power Which Is No Power"

I. God is Spirit, and if God is the creative principle of the universe, then this universe is a spiritual creation, not a physical one, not a corporeal one: a spiritual creation. If that is true, is it not foolish to pray to a spiritual God to do something to a physical universe which actually does not exist?

    A. We are dreaming when we are praying to a spiritual God to change some kind of matter, to change some physical structure. God is not in that picture.

    B. We need the practitioner who will sit down and realize that God is Spirit, the offspring of God is spiritual, and into that creation nothing enters that defileth or maketh a lie.

    C. Trying to change a material universe will get us nowhere spiritually.

II. Human mind broadcasting is not power. It can only be stopped by the realization of the nothingness and non-power of that which is claimed to be such great power.

    A. Look at some form of error—some form of sin or some form of disease or sick person—look right at it and say,

"Thou art not power; thou art carnal mind, or nothingness; thou art the arm of flesh, or nothingness. Thou couldst have no power unless it came from God, for there is no power but God." God is the life of all being, the immortality and the eternality. God is the only law, the only law-giver. There is no law of matter; there is no law of disease. Material power is not power; it is a claim of power. . . . God, Spirit, is power, and Spirit is infinite, Spirit is all-power.

B. Unless you are specific in your work, specific in your knowing of the truth, specific in your realization that you are being confronted with mental and physical powers that are not power, they will continue to be power until you have the realization of their non-power.

III. Reasons for lack of healing

A. The practitioner may. . . not be completely living, moving, and having his being in God-consciousness. . . . He does not rise high enough in consciousness to meet those more serious problems.

B. Sometimes it is because a practitioner has not the time to give to those cases that require years of work.

C. The patient has taken on some state of consciousness that just does not yield, does not give itself up, and those cases represent what appear to be our failures. . . . Even those who have seemed not to yield, if they were given enough time and enough work, eventually do.

IV. For most of our work, healing comes quickly, comes joyously. But the way of it is the realization that it is nothing but atheism to believe that material power is power. That is the secret of healing.

A. Spiritual power is the only real power. Any other claim of power can be reversed or nullified.

B. Material force is not power. Whether it appears as infection or contagion, whether it appears as mental hypnotism, it is the mind of flesh or the "arm of flesh," and it is, therefore, nothingness, for Spirit is the all and the real and the eternal.

C. Nullify every mental and physical claim of power wherever you meet up with it.

    1. Accept it as a responsibility that wherever your attention is drawn to mental or physical power, you will sit down, quietly and peacefully, and realize, "Not by might, nor by power, but by the spirit of God is all this made null and void."

    2. The invisible Spirit is the law and the cause of all that is. . . . Thank You, Father. This is Your universe, spiritual, complete.

V. The human mind is only an instrument that we use to lead us to a place where we no longer use it.

A. When the mind is not operating, that is when spiritual power is fully released.

B. The greatest healing works, the greatest works of restoration and reformation, the greatest works of spiritual power are accomplished when there is neither word nor thought, when there is a complete stillness. Then something takes place within, and that is the revelation of the Spirit and of the power of the Spirit.

C. There are no thoughts of the human mind that ever reach God. God reaches us in the silence, in the stillness, in the quietness.

VI. We must acknowledge that every finite concept is of the carnal mind, a sense of selfhood or power apart from God. But from there on, we go into the silence to realize that this that is appearing to us as the mind of man or the "arm of flesh" is not power, is not presence, is not law.

Study Guide and Excerpts from Joel S. Goldsmith's *1958 Second Sydney and Melbourne Closed Class*

About the Series

The 1971 through 1981 *Letters* will be published as a series of eleven fine-quality soft cover books. Each book published in the first edition will be offered by Acropolis Books and The Valor Foundation, and can be ordered from either source:

ACROPOLIS BOOKS, INC.
Distributed by
DEVORSS & COMPANY
PO Box 1389
Camarillo CA 93012
(800) 843-5743
www.devorss.com

THE VALOR FOUNDATION
1101 Hillcrest Drive
Hollywood, FL 33021
(954) 989-3000
www.valorfoundation.com

Scriptural References and Notes

CHAPTER ONE

1. Romans 8:17.
2. Luke 15:31.
3. Luke 12:22.
4. Psalm 23:4.
5. John 5:14.
6. Matthew 25:40.
7. Galatians 6:7.
8. Galatians 6:8.
9. John 8:11.
10. II Corinthians 12:9.
11. John 8:32.
12. Isaiah 2:22.
13. II Chronicles 32:8.
14. Isaiah 1:18.
15. Ezekiel 18:32.

CHAPTER TWO

1. Job 23:14.
2. Psalm 138:8.
3. Isaiah 45:2.
4. John 14:2.
5. Psalm 91:7.
6. Psalm 91:1.
7. II Corinthians 12:9.
8. Isaiah 1:18.
9. I John 4:4.
10. I Kings 19:12.
11. Galatians 2:20.
12. Hebrews 13:5.
13. Matthew 14:27.
14. John 8:58.
15. Matthew 28:20.
16. John 14:6.
17. Luke 12:22,30,32.
18. John 10:30.
19. Luke 15:31.

CHAPTER THREE

1. Isaiah 2:22.
2. John 10.30
3. By the author. (Acropolis Books. Atlanta, GA. 1997)
4. By the author. (Acropolis Books. Atlanta, GA. 1997)
5. Ecclesiastes 11:1.
6. Psalm 24:1.
7. Luke 15:31.
8. Matthew 4:4.
9. John 15:5.
10. John 6:35.
11. Psalm 127:1
12. Galatians 2:20.
13. Psalm 16:11.
14. Exodus 3:14.

CHAPTER FOUR

1. I Corinthians 2:14.
2. By the author. (Acropolis Books. Atlanta, GA. 1997)
3. By the author. (Harper Collins, New York, 1990)
4. By the author. (Acropolis Books. Atlanta, GA. 1997)
5. By the author. (Currently out of print.)
6. John 17:5.
7. John 10:30.
8. Romans 8:38,39.
9. John 20:2.
10. By the author. *The Infinite Way* (DeVorss & Company, 2002).
11. Exodus 3:14.
12. John 6:35.
13. John 4:32.
14. John 11:25.
15. Luke 15:31.
16. Hebrews 13:5.
17. Ephesians 5:14.

CHAPTER FIVE

1. Genesis 1:26.
2. John 18:36.
3. Romans 8:28.
4. Revelation 21:27.
5. Matthew 16:23.
6. Genesis 18:32.
7. John 6:35.
8. John 9:5.
9. John 14:6.
10. John 11:25.
11. II Chronicles 32:8.
12. Matthew 19:17.
13. John 5:30.
14. John 14:10.
15. Psalm 24:1.
16. Luke 15:31.

CHAPTER SIX

1. Isaiah 2:22.
2. John 8:32.
3. Matthew 5:14.
4. Matthew 19:21.
(Excerpt References:)
1. Isaiah 2:22.
2. Matthew 6:6.
3. John 10:30.
4. Matthew 6:6.

CHAPTER SEVEN

1. Matthew 16:16,17.
2. Romans 1:25.
3. Matthew 4:4.
4. Isaiah 45:2.
5. II Chronicles 20:15,17.
6. John 8:32.

CHAPTER EIGHT

1. John 8:32.
2. Luke 15:31.
3. Isaiah 2:22.
4. I Kings 17:13.
5. John 6:11.
6. Matthew 6:6.
7. By the author, *Our Spiritual Resources.*
8. Matthew 6:33.

CHAPTER NINE

1. John 4:24.
2. John 18:36.
3. John 5:30,31.
4. John 7:16.
5. John 14:10.
6. Ralph Waldo Emerson
7. By the author. *The Infinite Way* (DeVorss & Company, 2002).
8. *Ibid.*
9. Luke 15:31.
10. Matthew 6:32.
11. Luke 12:32.
12. Matthew 5:44,45.
13. Matthew 23:37.

CHAPTER TEN

1. Philippians 2:5.
2. Habakkuk 1:13.
3. I Corinthians 13:12.
4. I Corinthians 2:14.
5. Matthew 25:40.
6. John 10:30.
7. I Kings 19:12.
8. Matthew 24:44.
9. John 8:12.
10. Zechariah 4:6.
11. Isaiah 45:2.
12. John 14:2.

CHAPTER ELEVEN

1. John 7:24.
2. Matthew 19:17.
3. John 8:11.
4. Acts 10:34.
5. Matthew 5:23,24.
6. John 4:21.
7. Luke 17:20,21.
8. Exodus 3:14.
9. John 6:48.
10. John 11:25.
11. Psalm 23:1.
12. Psalm 91:1.

CHAPTER TWELVE

1. Psalm 91:1.
2. Psalm 23:4.
3. Joshua 24:15.
4. Psalm 19:1.
5. Psalm 118:24.
6. Matthew 23:9.
7. Hebrews 13:5.
8. Galatians 2:20.
9. Philippians 4:13.

TAPE RECORDED CLASSES CORRESPONDING TO
THE CHAPTERS OF THIS VOLUME

Tape recordings may be ordered from

THE INFINITE WAY
PO Box 8260
Moreno Valley, CA 92552 U.S.A.
Telephone 800-922-3195 Fax 951-656-1951
Email: info@joelgoldsmith.com
www.joelgoldsmith.com
Free Catalog upon Request

CHAPTER 1:   LIVING THE SPIRITUAL LIFE
               #370 *1960 Perth, Australia, Closed Class.*1:1,2

CHAPTER 2:   FROM PRACTICING THE PRESENCE TO THE
               PRAYER OF LISTENING
               #372 *1960 Perth, Australia, Closed Class.*3:1

CHAPTER 3:   MEDITATION, THE DOOR TO FULFILLMENT
               #302 *1960 Los Angeles, Closed Class.*2:2

CHAPTER 4:   THE STATURE OF SPIRITUAL MANHOOD
               #302 *1964 London, Closed Class.*1:1
               (This lesson, given Monday evening, June 15,
               1964, is Joel's last hour of classroom work
               before his transition, June 17, 1964.)

CHAPTER 5: NOTHING TAKES PLACE OUTSIDE OF
CONSCIOUSNESS
#302 *1960 Los Angeles Closed Class.* 2:1

CHAPTER 6: I, IF I BE LIFTED UP
#235 *1958 Manchester Closed Class.* 1:1,2

CHAPTER 7: A LESSON ON GRACE
#224 *1958 London Closed Class.* 1:1

CHAPTER 8: SPIRITUAL SUPPLY
#371 *1960 Perth, Australia, Closed Class.* 2:1

CHAPTER 9: CAST THY BREAD ON THE WATERS
#372 *1960 Perth, Australia, Closed Class.* 3:2

Chapter 10: The New Dispensation
#526 *1963 London Work; 2:1*
#512 *1963 Instructions for Teaching the Infinite
Way.* 5:1

CHAPTER 11: SELF-PURIFICATION, THE WAY TO THE MYSTICAL
CONSCIOUSNESS.
#267 *1959 Hawaiian Village Closed Class.*
6:1,2

CHAPTER 12: THE YE-SHALL-KNOW-THE-TRUTH WAY
#369 *1960 Maui Work.* 4:1